The Devil's Role in the Spiritual Life

The Devil's Role in the Spiritual Life

St. John of the Cross' Teaching on Satan's Involvement in Every Stage of Spiritual Growth

Cliff Ermatinger

Padre Pio Press   Milwaukee

Cover design by Ryan Rogers

© 2017 by Padre Pio Press, Milwaukee
All rights reserved
ISBN-13: 978-0692907238 (Padre Pio Press)

Printed in the United States of America

Dedication

To the Immaculate Heart of Mary on the 100th anniversary of her apparition at Fatima, with filial devotion.

Table of Contents

Introduction 1

- 1- St. John of the Cross: Life, Works, and Spirituality 5

-2- Synthesis of John's Thought on the Devil 12

-3- Spiritual Combat 19

-4- Essential Extraordinary Mystical Phenomenon 34

-5- Accidental Extraordinary Mystical Phenomena 57

-6- Diabolical Counterfeit Visions and Locutions 72

-7- The Devil's Strategies 97

-8- Diabolical Attacks on Those in the Purgative Stage 107

-9- Diabolical Attacks on Those in the Illuminative Stage 116

-10- Diabolical Attacks on Those in the Unitive Stage 134

Acknowledgments

Fr. William MacLean and the faithful Catholic community on the Isle of Skye who welcomed me with such warmth: *tapadh leibh!*

Thanks also to the Carmelite Sisters of the Monastery of the Holy Name in Denmark, WI who pray for me and always open their hermitage to me. Both communities offered me a haven where I could write this book in peace, surrounded by beauty, both created and uncreated.

Finally, thanks to Dave and Cecile Van Hecke, Michele Mazza, and Patrick Suth

*Be calm but vigilant, because your enemy the devil is prowling round
like a roaring lion, looking for someone to devour.*
I Pet 5:8

For even Satan himself disguises himself as an angel of light
II Cor 11:14

Introduction

Inspiration for this book

A newly ordained religious once mentioned to me in spiritual
direction that he felt called by God to devote more time to meditation
than his rule demanded. He was filled with delight and enthusiasm
as he envisioned this new venture. You might imagine his chagrin
when I offered for his consideration the possibility that this was
more than likely the work of the devil than of the divine Friend of
his soul. His rule was already demanding enough, and so was his
workload. "Not a problem", he said, "I'll get up earlier." I insisted
on my point. He reeled, letting me know what he thought of me,
which was fine. My concern was not that he like me, but for his
spiritual well-being. I reminded him of the ancient Greek saying,
Poly den einai polloi ("much, not many" or quality over quantity, for
a less literal translation). A curt "Thank you" was his response.

As suspected, the bubbly enthusiasm waned. In time, he became increasingly exhausted from his sleep deprivation; the long hours of prayer, once so sweet, were now burdensome. Soon, he had trouble fulfilling what his rule prescribed. All of this (the fatigue, the lack of prayer, general imbalance in his life) set him up for quite a fall in the moral sphere.

The devil, so it seems, takes the long view. He's willing to work subtly on a well-intentioned person and see how it plays out, lending a guiding hand along the way that, to an inexperienced person, seems divine. After all, how could the devil suggest more prayer? If it will serve his ends, he's all in.

The fact that a fervent religious was not capable of recognizing the devil's hand in his own spiritual disaster is made all the more poignant when we consider the multiplicity of demonic imagery that surrounds us. There is an ever-increasing and unhealthy curiosity for all things demonic. Movies, cartoons, apps, tattoos, clothing, games, music, videos, … little seems to escape being co-opted by those who want to peddle depictions of the Evil One. Yet, it seems that the more his representations multiply, the less we know about him and how he operates.

With a proportionalism that seems to approach exactitude, while Modernist theology dismissed belief in the devil, worldlings took it up – but without the context of sound theological principles. Hence, the caricature-like representations just mentioned.

It may seem counter-intuitive that the saints know much more about Satan than the most dedicated Satanists do, but so it is. The more one falls in love with Christ, the clearer the meaning of sin and the action of the one who inspires it becomes. So much for the saints….. About the rest of us, with heartfelt sentiments, St. John of the Cross complains: "And it is therefore greatly to be lamented that many who engage in this spiritual battle against the beast do not even destroy its first head by denying themselves the sensual things of the world."[1]

It is indeed sorrowful that some of us, many under vows or even ordained, live a disassociated life, forgetful of, or simply blind, to demonic activity in our spiritual lives. As a result, we are not awake to the subtle – and often not so subtle – diabolical interventions. Perhaps some will admit the devil's existence, but, as St. John says, are woefully ignorant of his ways. For others, perhaps, practically speaking, this reality remains something of an embarrassing element of Catholic doctrine and, if brought up in conversation, it is met with a paternalistic smile or an awkward silence and a quick change of subject.

Our Lord was not a psychologically weak and deluded individual when he went into combat with the demon in the desert. Scripture speaks of the devil's existence as a fact, not as a cultural convention to explain something else. He knew how to deal with the Father of Lies, dismissing him while keeping his gaze on the Father's most holy will. For the rest of us, the devil, so says St. Peter, *prowls around as a roaring lion looking for someone to devour* (*I Pet* 5:8). To live in denial of this fact, or ignorance of how to recognize his action, makes the work of the Adversary that much easier.

Layout of the book

After some cursory remarks about St. John of the Cross' life and spirituality (chapter 1), we look at a synthesis of his teachings on diabolical activity (chapter 2). In chapter 3, we consider some guiding principles that St. John has laid down regarding spiritual combat and the various contenders involved. We interrupt our Sanjuanistic study to present an *excursus* of elements of spiritual theology and what it teaches us about essential and accidental mystical phenomena (chapters 4 and 5). Following that, we take a detailed look at St. John's presentation of those phenomena and the devil's stratagems in counterfeiting them (chapters 6 and 7). The last three chapters discuss the nature of the devil's attacks on people in the three stages of the interior life, namely: beginners, proficient, and the perfect.

This book has benefited from the richness of its Sanjuanist and Teresian primary sources. It also draws from the voluminous writings that came out of the Carmelite Congress in Madrid, 1923. An article by Friar Nil de Saint-Brocard, OCD entitled "Il Demonio e Vita Spirituale", published in *Sanjuanisica*, in Rome, 1943 is another indispensible source. Of course, the sound principles of St. Thomas Aquinas and that spiritual treasure, *Dizionario di Mistica,* keep us grounded, as well.

It is my ardent hope that the observations, experience, and counsels of the Mystical Doctor alert the reader to the wiles of the Evil One in order to overcome him – not with one's own gifts and strength - but with faces turned towards Christ and ever growing abandonment to him.

Milwaukee
July 16th, 2017
Feast of Our Lady of Mount Carmel

- 1-

St. John of the Cross: Life, Works, and Spirituality

His Life

John of the Cross (baptized Juan de Yepes y Alvarez), it seems, was born to suffer. The youngest of three children in a small Avila town called Fontiveros enjoyed a few carefree years of the early 1540's before everything came crumbling down around him.

The relatively small family of five – of which John was the youngest – would be reduced to three while he was still young. The loss of his father (who had married below his own family's social state) meant the destitution of the young widow and her children who were turned away at the door of her in-laws. Shortly afterwards, John's infant brother would join their father in eternity, the victim of malnutrition.

After some years of witnessing his mother's journeying across Spain in search of scraps of food and whatever employ was to be had, John, in his turn, was soon old enough to make his own search for sustenance to support his mother. It was during this time that he found a stable position in the Hospital of Medina del Campo, caring for the infirm, changing them, cleaning them, loving them in their indigence and helplessness. Although he also needed the money to study at some point in the future, at the hospital, he was already receiving his most formative lessons among the suffering – experiences that would leave a life-long mark on his soul and psychology. John learned that poverty need not be a curse but could be lived out as a virtue – a necessary virtue, in fact, for union with his Beloved.

He studied for a while with the Jesuits. But in 1563 he surprised everyone who knew him by joining the Carmelite Fathers, taking the name Friar John of St. Matthias. John was devoted to the Blessed Virgin Mary and had a prodigious capacity for contemplation – to be a Carmelite made sense to him.

After his profession, he went to that great university city, Salamanca – something of the incense belt of Western Europe with practically every prominent religious order represented there. Not everything went as John had hoped. His contemplative longings were not satisfied and he was tempted to join the semi-hermit order of the Carthusians, but a providential encounter with Teresa of Avila quickly changed that plan. She had other plans for him. So did our Lord.

He joined Teresa in her reform of the Carmelites, changing his name to Friar John of the Cross on November 28th, 1568. The first years in the reform were something of a spiritual honeymoon for him. Everything smiled on him: he had lots of time for prayer and ministered to the poor and destitute of the surrounding villages. He was entrusted with some important positions: confessor to the nuns at Avila and novice master for the male branch of the order. Yet in 1577 something happened that would change his life radically.

He was taken captive by Carmelites who resisted Teresa's return to the primitive observance, seeing John as one of their primary threats. Nine months in a tiny, dank, stinking cell. This period would mark his soul more deeply than the wretchedness he found at Medina del Campo. He writes: "Only one grace of all the ones God granted me in that place could not be paid for in a cramped prison – even were I to spend years there." He says his experience of God's love was so profound its effect was that of a wound.

Wounded by the love of God, he could only be healed by the cautery of divine union. As a result he did what those with the mystic charism have always done: he described his experience through verse - some of the most sublime of all Spanish literature: 10 trinitarian romances, a poetic commentary on the *Song of Songs,* and a poem called "The Fountain."

He managed to escape prison – where he had been denied the sacraments, starved, covered in lice, and taken out of his hole to be whipped every Friday in the friary's refectory. He continued the work of the reform as a superior and educator, writing four major commentaries on his poetry: *The Ascent of Mount Carmel* (A), *The Dark Night of the Soul* (DN), *The Spiritual Canticle* (SC), and *The Living Flame of Love* (LF).

In 1591, on account of some calumnies, he was relieved of duty and was to be sent to the Mexican mission but ended up too sick to travel. He was then exiled to Andalucia, permitted to choose from several friaries in the region. The choice required little discernment: he quickly declared that he wanted the poorest house to be his home. He arrived sick and exhausted, received by the superior, Friar Diego Evangelista, who made Friar John understand what an onerous burden he was to the community. The superior hoped John wouldn't eat very much. Not much danger of that with Friar John, as he would later witness. He died there in 1591 on December 14th. Friar Diego moved by John's humble submission to his abuse during that period, and witnessing his holy death, repented.

His Works

"So that what I am about to say is more worthy of faith, I say nothing on my own authority - other than trusting my own experience and that which other spiritual persons have recounted. Yet, even though some might benefit from this it must all be confirmed and clarified with the authority of Sacred Scripture," says St. John in the prologue of *Spiritual Canticle*. John recognizes the primacy of Sacred Scripture over personal experience or that of other spiritual masters. Throughout his 2,500 poetic verses and thousands of pages of prose, one discovers a Thomistic and, therefore, Scholastic formation at the foundation, with frequent references to Augustine, Pseudo-Dionysius, and other prominent mystical writers from the Iberic Peninsula such as Teresa, Osuna, and Laredo. His works can be divided accordingly:

Minor works: 30 poems, of which 10 are romances; 5 glosses; *Maxims and Counsels; Degrees of Perfection; Sayings of Light and Love; Other Counsels*. John's poetry is the foundation and centerpiece of his work since, as he says, "commentary on them will always be inadequate to express the content of the inspired word."

Major works: *The Ascent of Mount Carmel* (in three books) describes the ascetical purification of the senses through the active way; the purification of the spiritual faculty of the intellect; and the purification of the memory and the will. *The Dark Night of the Soul* (in two books) examines the passive purification of the senses and of the spirit. This follows on the heels of *The Ascent*, something of a sequel. *The Spiritual Canticle* comments on four strophes revealing a spirituality of mystical marriage as a journey of conversion to full union with God, enduring purifications and entering into spousal communion with Christ's Sacred Humanity. *The Living Flame of Love* also comments on four strophes of the poem and discusses the *theosis* – the transformation of man into God by participation as an anticipation of glory.

Mystical Doctrine[2]

Rather than a theoretical or even a dogmatic theology, John's is an experiential, lived theology, more commonly referred to today as spiritual theology. His teaching is an ongoing hymn to the union with God, imparting it through poetry, letters, all founded on sound Scholastic principles. Perhaps he is best known for his teaching on the dark night, something he saw as worthy of his guidance for the readers since, "so little has been said about this and few have had the experience."[3]

For John, the mystical experience is above all immediacy of mystery. "In this high state of union, God does not communicate to the soul by way of anything sensed, such as imaginary visions, or similar figures; nor does he communicate through lips but mouth to mouth; that is, the naked and pure essence of God."[4] This union is granted "in the substance of the spirit, in the heart of the of the soul, as it were."[5] It is here where man is all passivity and receptivity: "where the Holy Spirit accomplishes all that he does and towards which he moves the soul."[6] The soul ought to "rest in God with loving attention, with a stilled intellect, almost as if it did nothing."[7]

Rarely does John use the word "sin". Rather he speaks in terms of appetites. Infrequently does John use the word "perfection", preferring other terms such as "union," or the "divine conjunction and union of the soul with the divine substance."[8] He presents the encounter between God and the soul in vivid and dynamic terms, distinguishing between the types of union: union through essence, through grace and spiritual affection; and union through similarity.[9] The first of which is natural, the latter two are supernatural gifts. Union is only granted through the intervention of God the Father who has ordered his creation toward conformity with his Son:[10] he created the world, humanity (and within that is the Church) as spouse for the Divine Word.[11] This spouse, is meant to be borne by him into a tender Trinitarian rapport of love by way of an exchange of nuptial gifts. This exchange occurs in the Incarnation.[12] As a result, there is a human element in this union which comes about "by way of perfection, little by little, at the soul's pace."[13]

Man is first attracted by the longing for God and responds by gradually emptying himself of everything that is not God, "because to love is to go about emptying oneself and stripping oneself of all that is not God in order to be for God." Man learns to act and constantly desire to imitate Christ in these actions, remaining empty of all for the love of Christ to such an extent that he not seek pleasure in anything so as to enjoy everything; to know nothing so as to know all.[14]

The Trinitarian and Christological Dimension of Mystical Union

Mystical union is communion with the Blessed Trinity. The Father is the principle Lover,[15] the Holy Spirit is the Guide and operative Agent in the soul,[16] and Christ is the Beloved, the Spouse and through love and conformity man is then divinized. Christ is brother, companion, teacher, reward, friend, and spouse, always present throughout the entire spiritual itinerary. At the beginning of the journey,[17] in the moment of all-important decisions,[18] as the one Word[19] in spousal union.[20] There, where the lover seeks the gaze of his only Love, is he opened up to the beauty of the world emanating from his divine glance.

Beyond the world of the senses, analogously, there exists a tripartite structure which finds its complement in the theological virtues: "The soul is united to God, in this life, by means of… faith according to the intellect, hope according to memory, and love according to the will."[21] The theological virtues are the means proportionate to the end of the union with God because they put us in contact with God himself and possess the mystical character of the receptivity.

John's spirituality recognizes God as the "center of the soul,"[22] whose only source of health is the love of God,[23] and which lives in the person whom it loves more than in the body it inhabits.[24]

Concluding the *Spiritual Canticle,* the saint exclaims: "O souls created for such greatness, and called to it, what are you doing? Your aspirations are too poor and your possessions miserable. O miserable blindness of the eyes of your soul because you are blind before such light and deaf to the voice. Without realizing you go in search of greatness and glory yet remain wretched and vile, ignorant and unworthy of so much good."[25]

-2-

Synthesis of John's Thought on the Devil in the Spiritual Life

John's teaching on the devil's role in the spiritual life reveals a man of much experience and wisdom. His teaching is rich in content, solid in its principles, and thorough in its detailed exposition.

John presents us with an integral vision of the spiritual life. Therefore, it is neither narrow, partial, nor shallow. Just as a healthy spiritual life includes beautiful encounters with the Beloved, it cannot lack assaults, traps, and temptations from the Evil One. John's teaching is not limited to lyrical expressions under inspiration of the Holy Spirit, but he has taken pains to include the experience of contemplative souls under the influence of the evil spirit throughout the gradual development of their spiritual activity. In other words, rather than appear as something paradoxical within the spiritual experience, this is something John presents as a given and is in full accord with the normal laws that govern the harmonic development of the spiritual life.

Throughout the entire Sanjuanistic spiritual itinerary one finds a malicious figure accompanying the soul. Just as Satan pursues and appears at the most salient moments in the life of Christ: he inspires Herod to kill the new born Christ-Child, he appears in an extraordinary fashion to our Lord at the inauguration of his public life during the temptations in the desert, he interrupts our Lord's preaching in the synagogue, manifests himself in a child immediately after Christ has been called *my beloved Son* in the Transfiguration, inspires Peter to tempt Christ away from the Cross (*Get behind me, Satan!*), creates havoc among the Apostles during the most sublime moments of the Last Supper by bringing them to bicker among themselves – to the point of possessing Judas moments later, and, of course, he was the puppet master of the sham trial and subsequent torture and death of Christ.

Satan and his countless minions are a reality found in Scripture, Magisterium, and Catholic Tradition, so too, in John's mystical journey. The devil remains – save for the final phase – a constant presence. With acute intelligence and twisted will this enemy – always with permission according to divine wisdom, providence, and justice – exercises infiltration of the intellective faculties and the internal as well as external appetites of the soul. What fills these demons with dread is that the person who anxiously strives towards its Beloved may actually arrive to the point of transforming union: the peak of the Holy Mountain.

The entire itinerary of the spiritual life includes this struggle against superior creatures, but creatures nonetheless. The *Catechism of the Catholic Church* says of the devil:

The power of Satan is, nonetheless, not infinite. He is only a creature, powerful from the fact that he is pure spirit, but still a creature. He cannot prevent the building up of God's reign. Although Satan may act in the world out of hatred for God and his kingdom in Christ Jesus, and although his action may cause grave injuries—of a spiritual nature and, indirectly, even of a physical nature—to each man and to society, the action is permitted by divine providence which with strength and gentleness guides human and cosmic history. It is a great mystery that providence should permit diabolical activity, but "we know that in everything God works for good with those who love him."[26]

The arts and tactics employed by demons have relative efficacy. In the beginning, the demon's work is almost imperceptible to the object of his attacks. As the soul progresses, the demon becomes more nervous and his activity more accentuated.

Faced with the demon's wiles, the contemplative soul must be trained in how to respond in order to neutralize their effects. This training, according to our mystical author, must be founded on the firm rock of *nada* – nothing. In other words, learning of the nothingness of everything created in order to be open to the All of Christ. The sense must be re-ordered by mortification and the soul must be exercised in theological virtue – and all of this sustained by that virtue which makes saints or reveals mediocrity: humility.

St. John of the Cross is only concerned with the essentials. And his spiritual doctrine is an exercise in the essentials of following Christ in order to be configured with him. Nonetheless, the Mystical Doctor writes from his own experience and the knowledge accrued from directing many souls along the way of holiness. He sets out a descriptive pattern of what generally happens. When he is prescriptive, it is quite obvious. Nonetheless, the particulars of transformation as described by St. John are not all replicated in every case without exceptions and attenuations. Rather, he lays out what usually occurs in great detail so much so that many who have taken to this path recognize much of themselves in his writing.

St. John of the Cross never intended his teaching on demonic involvement in man's spiritual life to be systematic. Nor was his intention to produce a treatise on demonology with all of its parts logically connected and coordinated. Nonetheless, extracting from the entire Sanjuanistic *corpus* every reference to demonic activity, as has been done for this book, one finds a logic and a cohesive unity to it all.

This unity which directs his teaching is latent, and not explicit. In order to trace these lines of demonic involvement in his teaching one must not stay on the surface, considering a few of the particulars. Rather, re-reading his entire works through this prism one discovers an organic treatment of this subject, laid out in solid, convincing terms and in a logical presentation. And as always, St. John of the Cross is eminently practical.

There is a central idea that unifies and directs the multiple manifestations of the dynamics imparted by Sanjuanistic thought. It regards the "point of weakness," addressed by both protagonists in the fight; i.e., the strategic movement upon which hinges both offensive and defensive maneuvers – the weakest and least resistant aspects of both contenders.

The two poles of weakness are: the weak point of the human soul with its natural inclination toward things sensible; and the devil's weakness – his inability to reach or even see what is occurring in the depths of the human soul. These two weaknesses will define and moderate the battle. For his part, the devil will most assuredly attack the lower aspects of the soul with ideas, discourses, images, and sensible attractions. The person under attack, on the other hand, will have to learn how to conduct himself so as not to be seduced by the interior and exterior impressions he experiences at the hands of his adversary. He will have to learn to hide himself in the depths of his soul, safe in contemplation.

These principles will determine the outcome of the battle. If a person opts to live a life in obedience to the senses, the devil will certainly vanquish him. If the person chooses to be a man of grace, silent recollection, and prayer, dwelling where the devil cannot reach him, he will be the victor.

These principles give sanjuanistic doctrine its vigor, excitement, and solidity. They are not dependent upon external and weak contingencies, but on the intimate and immutable nature of things as they are. In fact, the tendency towards sensible things results from our anthropology: man is a *suppositum* – a single nature – constituted of body and soul. The inability of the devil to see or work directly on the substance of the human soul derives from the fact that he, too, is a creature, limited in his scope. To know the thoughts and the very heart of man is reserved to man's Maker.

The Mystical Doctor adds nothing to our doctrinal knowledge of the devil that was not already present in seed form: he is called the Ancient Serpent, the Adversary, Tempter, Liar, Murderer, and one who transforms into an angel of light. What St. John of the Cross presents comes from experience. Lots of experience.

Only once in all of his writings does he refer to his own experience, albeit obliquely, with the devil, saying, "of this we have much experience."[27] On the other hand, his clinical eye in dealing with diabolical interventions in man's spiritual life reveals that what he calls "much experience" is just that. The Church does not call him the Mystical Doctor because he has read a lot about the subject. Sanjuanistic theology is nothing if not experiential theology, a lived faith. There is nothing too speculative about it. If he is writing about diabolical interventions at every stage of the spiritual itinerary it is precisely because he has "much experience."

It ought to interest us what his contemporaries relate about St. John's experience: "The demons went about at night, rabidly and angrily beating and landing many blows on the Saint."[28] This occurred while he was working as confessor in the Teresian convent of the Incarnation in Avila. It is also related that some observers could see the demons at times.[29]

St Teresa of Avila recounts in a letter what St. John has told her. He claimed that "it seemed as if the Lord had given the devil license to do all in his power against me" while he was held prisoner in Toledo.[30]

Beyond direct blows from the devil, our author was also on the receiving end of no less painful indirect demonic activity through human agents. The treatment he received in prison, some of the superiors who were unnaturally cruel to him, the accusations levied against him, - especially the infamous conduct of Friar Diego Evangelista, the superior of St. John' last community who insulted, neglected, and accused the saint mercilessly – can, without exaggeration, be attributed to the work of the Evil One.

None of this should surprise us when we consider that others – certainly demons – saw him as a terror of demons. Friar Martin of St. Joseph says that John of the Cross "imperiously made demons obey him."[31] Friar Alonso of the Mother of God relates that while St. John of the Cross heard confessions at the Church of the Holy Martyrs in Granada, demons under varying forms disturbed those at prayer and attempted to keep people from confessing with our author.[32]

St. Teresa of Avila, a practical woman not given to suggestion or sensationalism describes how the Lord gave St. John the power to exorcise demons from those people entrusted to his care. "John of the Cross has a special gift to cast out demons . . . In Avila he cast many from a person, and he commanded them in the name of God to tell him their names, and they obeyed immediately."[33] And elsewhere she relates, "Just now, he expelled three legions of demons from a person in Avila."[34] The process for John's canonical process of beatification and canonization concur with St. Teresa,[35] in which a long list of people, under oath, declared themselves witnesses to the saint's charisms and graces in dealing with demons.

In light of his firsthand experience and the particular call and gifts our Lord gave to St. John of the Cross – and his heroic generosity in cooperating with that grace - we can have no better guide in this often-murky field in which there are few experts.

He founds his teaching on the revealed Word of God, a vast knowledge of human psychology, and his singular experience with demons. It cannot be anything but solid and helpful.

-3-
Spiritual Combat

The Enemies of our Spiritual Life

In conformity with Catholic Tradition, St. John of the Cross recognizes our enemies as: "the world, the flesh, and the devil, who war against us, making the spiritual life difficult."[36] He makes this distinction: "the world is the most dangerous of enemies; the devil is the most difficult to unmask, while the flesh fights the hardest of all, making assaults that accompany a man into his old age."[37] All three must be defeated. "In order to vanquish one of these enemies, all three must be defeated. Once one is weakened, the other two lose their grip, and once all three have been overcome the soul has no more battles to fight."[38]

The World

At the beginning of *The Ascent of Mount Carmel*, St. John says, "all created things, compared to the infinite Being of God, are nothing (*nada*).[39] This recognition of the nothingness of creatures bears within itself the call to detach ourselves from them.

Our Spanish mystic uses the word "world" in two senses. The first sense is pejorative – much in the same way St. John the

Evangelist uses the term: an evil influence at odds with the Creator. The second sense of the word regards its finitude. This double sense of the term implies a double tension for the soul: on the one hand it consists of fleeing what is evil in the world; and on the other hand, recognizing the passing nature of the created (and its relative goodness) so as not to give oneself over to it at the cost of one's relationship with the Creator.

Those who surrender their affections to things of this world "become despicable, miserable, and impoverished through the love they offer the world, having it for beautiful and rich."[40] The riches of this world are at odds with divine Wisdom.

> The world is the wild beasts, because in the beginning of the heavenly journey the imagination pictures the world to the soul as wild beasts, threatening and fierce, principally in three ways. The first is, we must forfeit the world's favor, lose friends, credit, reputation, and property; the second is not less cruel: we must suffer the perpetual deprivation of all the comforts and pleasures of the world; and the third is still worse: evil tongues will rise against us, mock us, and speak of us with contempt. This strikes some persons so vividly that it becomes most difficult for them, I do not say to persevere, but even to enter on this road at all.[41]

For St. John, the words of St. James were a constant point of reference: *do you not know that the friendship with this world is enmity with God?"* (4:4). In form of protection against the wiles of the world, St. John of the Cross presents us with three counsels. The first is:

> you should have an equal love for and an equal forgetfulness

of all persons, whether relatives or not, and withdraw your heart from relatives as much as from others, and in some ways even more for fear that flesh and blood might be quickened by the natural love that is ever alive among kin and must always be mortified for the sake of spiritual perfection.[42]

The second is:

The precaution against the world concerns temporal goods. To free yourself truly of the harm stemming from this kind of good and to moderate the excess of your appetite, you should abhor all manner of possessions and not allow yourself to worry about these goods, neither for food, nor for clothing, nor for any other created thing, nor for tomorrow, and direct this care to something higher -- to seeking the kingdom of God (seeking not to fail God); and the rest, as His Majesty says, will be added unto us (Mt. 6:33), for he who looks after the beasts will not be forgetful of you. By this practice you will attain silence and peace in the senses.[43]

And the third is:

It is that you very carefully guard yourself against thinking about what happens (around you), and even more against speaking of it, of anything in the past or present concerning a particular (person): nothing about his or her character or conduct or deeds no matter how serious any of this seems. Do not say anything out of zeal or of desire to be right, unless at the proper time to whomever by right you ought to tell. Never be scandalized or astonished at anything you happen to see or learn of, endeavoring to preserve your soul in forgetfulness of all that.

For, should you desire to pay heed to things, many will seem wrong, even were you to live among angels, because of your not understanding the substance of them. Take Lot's wife as an example: Because she was troubled at the destruction of the sodomites and turned her head to watch what was happening, God punished her by converting her into a pillar of salt (Gen 19:26). You are thus to understand God's will: that even were you to live among devils you should not turn the head of your thoughts to their affairs but forget these things entirely and strive to keep your soul occupied purely and entirely in God, and not let the thought of this thing or that hinder you from so doing.

And to achieve this, be convinced that in monasteries and communities there is never a lack of stumbling blocks, since there is never a lack of devils who seek to overthrow the saints; God permits this in order to prove and try religious.

And if you do not guard yourself, acting as though you were not in the house, you will not know how to be a religious no matter how much you do, nor will you attain holy denudation and recollection or free yourself of the harm arising from these thoughts. If you are not cautious in this manner, no matter how good your intention and zeal, the devil will catch you in one way or another. And you are already fully captive when you allow yourself distractions of this sort.

Recall what the Apostle St. James asserts: *If anyone thinks he is religious, not restraining the tongue, that one's religion is vain*

(1:26). This applies as much to the interior as to the exterior tongue.[44]

The Flesh

Flesh, for St. John of the Cross, means concupiscence and sensuality:

> [T]hese are the natural resistance and rebellion of the flesh against the spirit, for, as St. Paul says, the *flesh lusts against the spirit* (Gal 5:17) and sets itself as a frontier against the soul on its spiritual road. This frontier the soul must cross, surmounting difficulties, and trampling underfoot all sensual appetites and all natural affections with great courage and resolution of spirit: for while they remain in the soul, the spirit will be hindered by them and not advance to the true life and spiritual delight. This is set clearly before us by St. Paul, saying: *If by the spirit you mortify the deeds of the flesh, you shall live* (Rom 8:13).

Flesh also means all the disorder that is within man, above that of the will, bringing man to love himself over God. Throughout St. John's writings, this disorder is roundly criticized in the form of the disorder of seeking peace and spiritual consolation as an end in itself:

> To free oneself from all temporal things, but even beyond that, to not allow oneself to be seduced by spiritual goods and remain in that perfect spiritual indigence is indispensable for union with God.[45]

The carnal man acts according to his desires, since the flesh is rooted in appetites. "This is the source of all sensuality which feeds concupiscence".[46] Citing Paul's doctrine that *the flesh lusts against the spirit* St. John of the Cross tells us that he who remains in the flesh also involves the spirit in his own downfall because:

> It is also evident regarding spiritual lust that through the sensory dryness and distaste experienced in its exercises, the soul is freed of those impurities already noted. For we said that they ordinarily proceed from the delight of the spirit in the senses.[47]

Further, he says:

> Desire blinds and darkens the soul; for desire, as such, is blind, since of itself it has no understanding in itself, the reason being to it always, as it were, a child leading a blind man. And hence it comes to pass that, whenever the soul is guided by its desire, it becomes blind; for this is as if one that sees were guided by one that sees not, which is, as it were, for both to be blind.[48]

Thus, living according to the flesh, man reduces his ability to perceive the world around him correctly and, much less, those spiritual realities. His will shrinks to this dimension and, thus attached to the tangible world, he becomes incapable of a true relationship with God. The world and the flesh render a man a slave to the devil.

The Devil

Clearly, the devil uses the world and the flesh to his ends and all three of these things ultimately converge. Among those creatures God has created "by means of his wisdom, which is his only begotten Son, the Word,"[49] are the heavenly spirits or angels.[50] These are intelligent beings, far surpassing man in many qualities given their nature as pure spirits.[51] Nonetheless, they differ infinitely from God.[52] There is no angel, no matter how intelligent or eminent, that could stand before the Lord and compare with him in any way.[53]

Among these pure spirits are counted not only celestial spirits but also fallen and, therefore, evil spirits.[54] The good spirits we commonly call angels[55] while the evil spirits are commonly called demons[56] or Satan.[57]

> Evil spirits, the second enemy of the soul, are called mighty, because they strive with all their might to seize on the passes of the spiritual road; and because the temptations they suggest are harder to overcome, and the craft they employ more difficult to detect, than all the seductions of the world and the flesh; and because, also, they strengthen their own position by the help of the world and the flesh in order to fight vigorously against the soul.[58]

St. John encourages us to fight the good fight. We are, after all, in it till death. As a result, we may as well see it for what it is: a grace to be accepted and cooperated with. St. John refers to his sister in the spirit, St. Teresa's doctrine of the seven mansions and the demons that greet the soul in each one:

> Blessed the soul who engages in battle with the seven-headed beast of the Apocalypse, set over against these seven steps of love, and which makes war against each one, and strives thus against the soul in each of these mansions, wherein the soul is being exercised and is mounting step by step in the love of God. And undoubtedly if it strives faithfully against each of

these heads, and gain the victory, it will deserve to pass from one step to another, and from one mansion to another, even unto the last, leaving the beast vanquished after destroying its seven heads, wherewith it made so furious a war upon it.[59]

In order to have a more complete understanding we shall take a look at their intellectual capacities, their moral qualities, and their dealing with men.

Demonic Intellectual Capacity

As a pure spirit, a demon naturally has an acute brilliance and a capacity to know things that would be impossible for man to grasp.[60]

[F]or in his converse with the soul the devil habitually wears the same guise as God assumes in His dealings with it, setting before it things that are very like to those which God communicates to it, insinuating himself, like the wolf in sheep's clothing, among the flock, with a success so nearly complete that he can hardly be recognized. For, since he says many things that are true, and in conformity with reason, and things that come to pass as he describes them, it is very easy for the soul to be deceived, and to think that, since these things come to pass as he says, and the future is correctly foretold, this can be the work of none save God; for such souls know not that it is a very easy thing for one that has clear natural light to be acquainted, as to their causes, with things, or with many of them, which have been or shall be. And since the devil has a very clear light of this kind, he can very easily deduce effect from cause, although it may not always turn out as he says, because all causes depend upon the will of God.[61]

Regarding external events, for example, they can have a clear idea of when earthquakes and plagues will occur or even the length of someone's life.[62]

The devil knows that the constitution of the earth and the atmosphere, and the laws ruling the sun, are disposed in such manner and in such degree that, when a certain moment has arrived, it will necessarily follow, according to the laws of nature laid down for these elements, that they will infect people with pestilence, and he knows in what places this will be more severe and in what places less so. Here you have a knowledge of pestilence in respect of its causes. What a wonderful thing it seems when the devil reveals this to a soul, saying: 'In a year or in six months from now there will be pestilence,' and it happens as he says! And yet this is a prophecy of the devil. In the same way he may have a knowledge of earthquakes, and, seeing that the bowels of the earth are filling with air, will say: 'At such a time there will be an earthquake.' Yet this is only natural knowledge...[63]

Our Spanish mystic goes on to say:

And likewise, supernatural events and happenings may be known, in their causes, in matters concerning Divine Providence, which deals most justly and surely as is required by their good or evil causes as regards the sons of men. For one may know by natural means that such or such a person, or such or such a city, or some other place, is in such or such necessity, or has reached such or such a point, so that God, according to His providence and justice, must deal with such a person or thing in the way required by its cause, and in the way that is fitting for it, whether by means of punishment or of reward, as the cause merits. And then one can say: 'Most certainly at such a time God will give you this, or will do this, or that will come to pass.' It was this that holy Judith said to Holofernes, when, in order to persuade him that the children of Israel would without fail be destroyed, she first related to him many of their sins and the evil deeds that they did. And then she said: *Since they do these things, it is certain that they will be destroyed* (Jud 11:12). This is to know the punishment in the cause, and it is as though she had said: It is certain that such sins must be the cause of such punishments, at the hand of God Who is most just. And as the Divine Wisdom says: *With respect to that and for that wherein a man sins, therein is he punished* (11:17).

The devil may have knowledge of this, not only naturally, but also by the experience which he has of having seen God do similar things, and he can foretell it and do so correctly. Again, holy Tobias was aware of the punishment of the city of Niniveh because of its cause, and he thus admonished his son, saying: *Behold, son, in the hour when your mother and I die, leave this land, for it will not remain. I see clearly that its own iniquity will be the cause of its punishment, which will be that it shall be ended and destroyed altogether* (Tob 24:13). This might have been known by the devil as well as by Tobias, not only because of the iniquity of the city, but by experience, since they had seen that for the sins of the world God destroyed it in the Flood, and that the Sodomites, too, perished for their sins by fire; but Tobias knew it also through the Divine Spirit.[64]

The Devil in the Spiritual Life

With regard to human psychology, a demon can, with relative accuracy, naturally foresee words, movements, and other signs of this sort, and it becomes easier as he gets to know the talents, inclinations, and the hidden secrets within the intimacy of one's heart.[65] It should be noted that these exterior signs (words, inclinations, actions, etc.) are what reveals the interiority of man. No angel, except through divine revelation, can know the interior of man's mind and heart.[66]

In the moral and spiritual order, based on his ever-increasing experience and knowledge of the state of one's soul and taking into account what he has witnessed in divine intervention in similar circumstances,[67] Satan acquires an ability to foresee analogous divine interventions in the government of the world.[68] St. John says, "The Lord's providence most justly and certainly unfolds as demanded by the good and evil causes as regards the sons of men."[69] The cognitive power of evil spirits reaches to such subtle and intricate realities as these.[70]

"Knowing of events, even if only in their very beginnings, he can easily deduce certain effects from their causes.[71] As a result, it is this way that a demon can predict the future. It may appear as a demonic "prophecy."[72] But it would not be an authentic prophecy as it would not be infallible nor would it result to be so in every case. At the end of the day, demons have to guess.[73] Although St. Thomas says that "whoever knows a contingent effect in its cause only, has merely a conjectural knowledge of it."[74] Nevertheless, the unfolding of all secondary causes depends on the divine will.[75]

Further, in things regarding the area of the faith, such as those most intimate communications which God grants to generous souls, the devil finds his limit.[76] It could be that a demon gains knowledge of spiritual favors granted to a soul by means of a good angel[77] as these are so-called "spiritual communications".[78] Nonetheless, regarding those things that the Lord bestows directly to the soul, Satan is blind to their existence, their arrival, their nature. All he can do is conjecture from the immense silence and peace he witnesses in these people of quieted senses and the subdued appetites. From this profound calm he might deduce that the soul is enjoying particular divine favors.[79]

Yet when dealing with certain types of contemplation such as darkened prayer, also known as mystical theology,[80] involving those interior and secret communications described as "substantial touches" of divine union,[81] and those close, loving embraces between God and the soul,[82] the devil cannot know about them or what occurs within them: everything of this nature is unknown to him, "completely hidden and dark."[83]

Demonic Moral Structure and Qualities

As fallen angels we ought not think that they are essentially perverse. In their origins and their nature, all angels were created good. Entranced by their own beauty and self-sufficient in their own natural gifts, they became evil and were cast down into the abyss of hell.[84] In their present guilty state John calls them "evil," "malicious," "proud," "clever," and "envious" spirits.[85] Thus, retaining their good nature, they made themselves evil in their wills. "Their evil and viciousness is so deeply rooted that… they wear their evil like armor: ordered, joined to others, and organized, thus giving them tremendous strength and vigor to carry out their evil."[86]

On the other hand, there is also the profoundly perverse dominion he lords over certain people held tightly in his grip. Certainly, the devil is no stranger to our world, nor is he indifferent about how we operate; he watches and keeps an invariably hostile relationship with us.

Why such Diabolical Involvement with Man

It would be helpful to distinguish the *fact* of diabolic interference from the *motives* that justify it, as well as its breadth and flow. Satan is called the enemy of human nature. He is the "strong man"[87], against whom the banished, poor children of Eve can do nothing except in Jesus Christ, the Lord of heaven and earth. Before Christ opens to them the gates of heaven, he redeems them and frees them from the power of Satan.[88]

Although Satan is the enemy of all humanity, John says he is particularly hateful of the human soul.[89] <u>More than anything he wants people to fall into sin,</u>[90] and he focuses most of his attention on those people of spiritual greatness.[91] He also maintains that the devil is the darkest being imaginable[92] and nothing of this world can compare with him.[93] No human effort is enough to combat him, except with God's aid[94] and only the divine light can unmask his stratagems and overcome him.[95]

For sure, other enemies (world and flesh) attack the soul and oblige us to enter into spiritual combat.[96] The most common of them all is the flesh with all of its assaults – and this lasts into old age, inciting repulsion for spiritual things and rebellion.[97]

He calls devils, the second enemy, "strong men" because they strive mightily to entrap her on this road and also because their temptations are stronger and their wiles more baffling than those of the world and the flesh and, finally, because the devils reinforce themselves with these other two enemies, the world and the flesh, in order to wage a rugged war.

David, in alluding to them, calls them strong men: *The strong men sought after my soul* (Ps. 54:3). The prophet Job also remarked concerning this strength that there is no power on earth comparable to that of the devil, who was made to fear no one (Jb. 41:25); that is, no human strength is comparable to his. Only divine power is sufficient to conquer him and only divine light can understand his wiles.

A soul that must overcome the devil's strength will be unable to do so without prayer, nor will it be able to understand his deceits without mortification and humility. St. Paul counsels the faithful: *Put on the armor of God that you may be able to resist the wiles of the devil, for this struggle is not against flesh and blood* (Eph. 6:11-12]). By blood he means the world, and by the armor of God, prayer and the cross of Christ, in which are found the humility and mortification we mentioned.[98]

Further, St. John goes on to say that the devil uses the world and the flesh as his satellites in order to vanquish the human soul. St. Thomas agrees, saying that the Evil One uses "the flesh and the world as instrumental and material causes" of temptation.[99]

Beyond the basic garden-variety diabolical activity St. John describes, there are those who willfully submit themselves to a demonic alliance, making a pact with the devil. Sorcerers, witches, soothsayers, psychics, et al. enter into a sort of pact with the devil, usually led by the devil's pride and envy.

For, when the devil sees them attached to these things, he opens a wide field to them, gives them abundant material and interferes with them in many ways; whereupon they spread their sails and become shamelessly audacious in the freedom wherewith they work these marvels.

Nor does the evil stop here. To such a point does their joy in these works and their eagerness for them extend that, if before they had a secret compact with the devil (and many of them do in fact perform these works by such secret compacts), it now makes them bold enough to work with him by an explicit and manifest compact, submitting themselves to him, by agreement, as his disciples and allies.

Hence, we have wizards, enchanters, magicians, soothsayers and sorcerers. And so far does the joy of these persons in their works carry them that, not only do they seek to purchase gifts and graces with money, as did Simon Magus, in order to serve the devil, but they even strive to obtain sacred things, and (which cannot be said without trembling) Divine things, for even the very Body of our Lord Jesus Christ has been seen to be usurped for the use of their wicked deeds and abominations. May God here extend and show to them His great mercy![100]

-4-

General Guiding Principles Regarding the Essential Extraordinary Mystical Phenomenon

St. John is called "The Mystical Doctor" and rightfully so. No other writer has presented experiential spiritual theology with such clarity, depth, and structure.

Nonetheless, we run the danger of misunderstanding his teaching if we lack a proper understanding of terminology used to describe mystical phenomena, ending up with an eclectic set of experiences. Further, to discuss visions, locutions, and other such *accidental* extraordinary mystical phenomena without having a firm grasp of their context, namely, the *essential* extraordinary mystical phenomenon, is not helpful at all. The terminology, correctly understood, affords us a structure in which to understand what St. John of the Cross teaches us. As a starting point, all mystical phenomena, whether essential or accidental, has God as its immediate and sole cause.

Contemplation: The Essential Extraordinary Mystical Phenomenon

The essential phenomenon of all mystical life's most complex phenomenon is known to theologians by one word: contemplation. Contemplation is an infused prayer. A more adequate and complete formula should be this: the intimate union of the soul with God through infused prayer of contemplation.

Infused contemplation has nothing to do with the natural exercise of the intellectual faculties through reflection, discursive meditation or even contemplative prayer in the Ignatian sense.

Christian Perfection

The contemplative grace, when granted, is usually received by those who have attained a degree of Christian perfection. The union of the soul with God, ending in the happiness of Heaven, which is more or less vaguely anticipated on earth, is not exclusively and proper to the mystical life, but is common to all perfect life.

The earnest effort of the soul to approach God, to become united to him by a moral union of association; to bring about, as it were, fusion of our mind, heart, and will with the thoughts, affections, and good pleasure of God – in a word, to produce within ourselves an ever flowing stream of the divine life that are sown by faith, hope, and charity– this is the essential task of all Christian perfection. Union with God, then in our definition, is only the genus.

The specific difference of mystical union consists in the means or instrument of union offered by God in his merciful goodness, called in the definition infused prayer of contemplation. It is on this particular point, then, that any discussion of further mystical phenomena must be brought to bear. If this point is not clearly understood, we set ourselves up for all sorts of confusion. For greater clearness we shall first state what this mystical prayer is not; and then proceed to state what it is.

What Infused Contemplation is Not

According to all the masters of the spiritual life, prayer in the ordinary ways of Christian perfection has four degrees in its advance towards perfection. None of these, however, is as yet the infused prayer of contemplation, because, far from being passive for infused into the soul, they are the product of its personal efforts, assisted by the ordinary help of the grace of God.

Vocal Prayer: Those prayers recited more or less slowly and thoughtfully. This is the simplest degree, the most elementary of all: that of beginners.

Mental Prayer or Meditation: This degree of prayer pertains to somewhat more advanced beginners. It consists in a series of considerations on a given subject, according to a method that acts as a guide, and ends with practical reflections and resolutions. Its chief end is to enlighten and strengthen faith and to reform life. Here we can find help in Sanuanistic teaching: for instance, he includes as possible subjects for meditation not only scenes from the Gospels but also God "seated upon the throne with resplendent majesty"; or "the imagining and considering of glory has beautiful light"[101] as followers of Christ, we are invited to identify the lover in the *Song of Songs* with Jesus Christ. It is helpful in our meditation to read this most beautiful book of the Bible through the prism of divine nuptials. In it, one recognizes that the divine Initiator of this love story is also he who nurtures our life (6:3), heals our ills (1:3), delivers us from evil (2:10), and is the one with whom we can be familiar yet forever remains beyond our grasp (5:6).

In *The Spiritual Canticle*, stanzas 4 to 7, St. John of the Cross tells us that "this reflection on creatures, this observing that they are made by the very hand of God, her Beloved[102], strongly awakens the soul to love Him." In this prayer there is a primacy of the intellect and memory.

Affective Prayer: A type of prayer that only differs from the preceding in that more prominence is given to the affections of a heart and to the effort of the will. It has in view not so much of the enlightenment of the soul or the strengthening of its convictions, as the rousing (and subsequent purification) of its various emotions and the enkindling of divine love; above all, by means of holy colloquies with the Beloved.

Because we were made for more than rational discourse in discursive meditation, we are invited to seek God's presence within our souls. In the commentary to stanza 11.3 of *The Spiritual Canticle*, our author reveals this presence in three ways. There is a contingent presence of God in all of his creation, without which, all would fall into instant annihilation.

Secondly, God is present by grace in the hearts of all Christians whether they are consciously aware of it or not. This grace strengthens them to lovingly keep his commandments and militate against sin.

Thirdly, God's presence may be perceived by God's own action, willing that his presence be known. "This presence is so sublime that the soul feels an immense hidden being is there from which God communicates to her some semi – clear glimpses of his divine beauty. And these bear such an effect on the soul that she ardently longs and faints with desire for what she feels hidden there in that presence. This is similar to what David felt when he exclaimed: "My soul longs and faints for the courts of the Lord [Ps. 84:2]."[103]

My son, I will give myself

To him who loves you,
And I love him
With the same love I have for you,
Because he has loved
You Whom I so love.[104]

In this prayer there is a primacy of the will and the affections.

Persevering without hesitation, the heart is then prepared and purified by our Lord. As St. John of the Cross says, "My house being now stilled", God begins to take over the prayer and lead it in a more direct way. This is accompanied by the passive night of the senses. As a result, the person can advance to a deeper, simpler prayer.

Prayer of Simplicity or Simple Regard: This prayer is somewhat less-known than the others, and therefore requires explaining in greater detail, because it is occasionally labeled, in a wide sense, by the name contemplation or acquired contemplation. There is thus the risk of confounding it with mystical or contemplation, which, although a close neighbor, bordering perhaps, is nevertheless of quite another nature, because it is passive or infused, and is no longer, as are the preceding states, the fruit of labor aided by the ordinary help of divine grace.

In the prayer of simplicity, everything becomes simpler as intensity increases. The multiplicity of discursive considerations that belong to ordinary meditation come to a halt. A single idea suffices, and if there are still several, they are few in number and succeed one another more slowly, more gently, beneath a simple intuitive regard, in no way discursive. Long and complicated reasoning has no home here; the mind sees and contemplates without development of thought.

Similarly, there is no longer a series of complicated affections. One, sole affection suffices, in which the soul is, as it were, for a long time suspended, and if several follow each other, they are few, and become blended together in a seamless way. The result is, not indeed an involuntary passivity, imposed by God, or a ligature of all of our faculties, understanding, heart, and will as is the case with infused prayer; but a certain voluntary immobility or quiet, in a singular act of loving attention to the Beloved.

There is an imperceptible transition between the four degrees of prayer of which this is last and the highest. It is reached by a gradual process, because the law of continuity belongs to grace as it does to nature.

It is true that the prayer of simplicity, when prolonged, is not suitable for everyone, because all have not the same facility in its practice. This facility varies according to the character and natural dispositions of each one, and above all with his intellectual culture and mode of life. Furthermore, it is dangerous to attempt an imposition of this method of prayer on all souls without distinction or proper preparation, for all have not received the same number of talents.

Those with little memory or imagination are obliged to rest content with few words and few images, and thus show great aptitude for this simplified prayer. On the contrary, those with vivid imaginations and excitable temperaments experience great difficulty should they attempt this method of prayer - their minds are filled with the constant flood of memories, images, and emotions, which keep them in a state of continual flux and motion.

In the same way, simple souls without great learning and culture can sometimes find themselves, in God's presence with more facility, content with a few ideas in a deep sense of that presence. On the contrary, great theologians and preachers abound in ideas, reasons, and texts, and cannot settle down to this simplicity with ease. It is, above all, those of a loving and affectionate nature for whom this exercise, in which all is love without complicated reasons, has the greatest attraction.

Certain timorous souls, being once raised to the prayer of simplicity, may be inclined to doubt the utility of that state, in which they fear inaction, idleness, laziness, and waste of time. But this is mere appearance. One single action is not inaction; on the contrary, it is actually intensified, in which all the activities of the soul are concentrated on one point. In this prayer the same things are produced as in ordinary meditation, enlightenment of the mind, warmth of heart, and aspiration of will; they are produced in a simpler, gentler, and less apparent way. Interior labor is less noisy, makes less noise, less apparent from without. It is, nonetheless, a more real and intense work.

Souls raised to this simplicity of prayer must be aided and lead past difficulties and through the labor and aridity they must encounter on their path. Bossuet drew up a short method of making prayer in faith for the Visitation Sisters. St. Francis de Sales gave the rules for the prayer of simple yielding to God. St. Teresa also treated of the prayer of recollection. All of these are names for the prayer of simplicity.

None of the four degrees of prayer that we have briefly described are yet the infused prayer of contemplation, for this is an extraordinary grace and not simply a higher and more eminent degree of ordinary prayer. Otherwise contemplatives, when they enter this new way, would not have the sensation, so often described by them, of entrance into a sphere altogether new, astonishing, and comprehensible; but, on the contrary, they would have a feeling of what has been, at least in part, a former experience. They would not experience that anxiety, unrest, and tremor, which is almost always felt in the presence of the mysterious and unforeseen reality. Nor would they feel the utter need of an enlightened guidance, the lack of which was, for St. Teresa, such a long and cruel a martyrdom.

The science of mysticism itself would be considerably simplified. Instead of enormous volumes which the great teachers have devoted to it, and the endless discussions to which it has given rise, just a few lines would suffice in order for the reader to grasp the principles and ordinary rules of ascetic theology. For a new degree in faith and fervor, however high, would not be able to change essentially the principles and rules of Christian piety.

The Latin dictum is true here: *Plus aut minus non mutat speciem.* The difference here is not of degree but of species.

> [This] is a principal point, and because a soul, when our Lord begins to bestow these graces upon it, does not understand them, and does not know what to do with itself; for if God leads it by the way of fear, as He led me, its trial will be heavy, if there be no one who understands the state it is in."[105] It is the beginning of the great darkness.

Notice the difference between the ordinary workings of grace and the extraordinary workings of grace. Further we underline the distinction between those graces that are experiential – that is, we are aware of them, and those unconscious phenomena, which occur, unbeknownst to us.

For example, the divine action through the gifts of the Holy Spirit usually works unconsciously. Consequently, they could not be deemed mystical graces.

St. Teresa insists on knowledge of the experience as a necessary element: "Our Lord will have the soul to see, as it were, with the naked eye this particular help of grace." The contemplative soul is then conscious of being passive in the hands of God, of receiving into itself and infused power, raising it to supernatural and superhuman act of knowledge and of love. It is the sensation of the Divine or the experimental knowledge of the action of God in our souls.

Without this important distinction it would be necessary to declare that every action of the Holy Spirit is truly mystical, which would be incorrect. Otherwise, this would lead to the superficial distinction of classifying all work of the Holy Spirit as mystical, and all work of the virtue as ascetical. But this division is too simple and insufficient to explain the facts observed by St. Teresa. Moreover, it would bring us to strange conclusions, for since the gifts are necessary to all spiritual life, and can be granted to discursive prayers, as to prayers of simple regard, we should have infused and mystical meditations as well as infused contemplations. Further, the martyrs and virgins who exercise the gifts of fortitude to a heroic degree, and even all good Christians, docile to the inspirations of the Holy Spirit, would be classified as mystics unaware of the divine work.

From a practical point of view, the usefulness of such a division will be nonexistent; no director would be able to distinguish whether an action was due to a virtue or to a gift. We must, therefore, seek it elsewhere, outside the invisible and unconscious world, for the distinctive character belonging to mystical contemplation, after having thus eliminating those that have no claim to be so. So, what is it?

The Nature of Infused Contemplation

Light and infused love, obtained without reasoning. Infused contemplation is the mystical operation par excellence. It is the experimental knowledge of divine things or realities, produced by God supernaturally in the soul, and it is the state of closest approach and union between God and the soul that can be obtained in this life.

St. Thomas says: "Contemplation is a simple intellectual intuition of truth… ending in an affective movement of the heart."[106]

As an intuition it is not of the senses, but of the mind, comparable afar to the external senses in that they reach directly the end proper to them. It is a pure intuition, excluding all effort of seeking, all reasoning, all the stress of action, and may even exclude every sensible image, as we shall point out in its proper place. *Voluntas sequitur intellectum* (the will follows the intellect): it requires this sequence as an indispensable disposition and preparation. St. Thomas adds that it is a loving intuition.

Further, it is an experimental intuition, which attains like sensation, not an abstract, but a real and actual object, attains it directly, i.e., without any reasoning.

The object of this intuition, then, is transcendent, it is divine, and, as will be seen later according to St. Thomas, it is God himself obscurely perceived, not face-to-face and in his essence, but in his created action in our souls, as an agent is perceived in his action. We recognize God by his divine touch, as we recognize a friend in the darkness by the touch of his hand.

Finally, this intuition is passive, and St. Thomas rightly insists on this involuntary and conscious passiveness, which characterizes either the intuitive element or the affective element of contemplation and would alone be sufficient to distinguish it from all the fundamentally active exercises of the ascetic life. St. Teresa: "In vocal or mental prayer with the assistance of God's grace we can help ourselves to a certain extent; not so in contemplation: this is beyond our natural powers and he does all."[107]

St. John of the Cross says, "God communicates himself to the soul, thus passive, as the light of the sun to him his eyes are open."[108]

Similarly, Aquinas instructs:

In the lower degrees of prayer, the soul loves and is loved, seeks and is sought, calls and is called; but in this degree, by a wonderful and unspeakable process, it rises and is raised, seizes and is seized, presses closely and is tightly bound, and with the knot of love ties itself to God, being with him as the alone with the Alone."[109]

This phenomenon implies a higher light than that of the human intelligence; a light which is not the laborious product of the activity of the mind, an infused light, received passively by him who contemplates it; so that the mind of man is truly passive beneath the sway of this divine touch which penetrates and enlightens it, instructing it without labor.

Another element is the effective reaction of the heart and of the will, which produces wonder and a fire of love capable of fixing, binding, or spending all the other powers of the soul.

To sum up this doctrine in a word: mystical contemplation consists in an experimental sensation of the divine, that is, in an immediate intuition by the consciousness, more or less clear or obscure, of the presence in our souls of God or a supernatural object - the essence remaining unknown - which produces a sentiment of admiration and love, suspending more or less the powers of the soul.

So-called philosophical contemplation is of the natural order, while that of the mystical sort is wholly supernatural (has God as its motor). The former has as its object an idea, such as the idea of God; the second has the very reality of the active presence in us of the divine being. The former is produced by the reasoning or intuitive effort of man's genius; the second is a gift of God and the product of his supernatural action in the soul of his choosing.

Meditation seeks, contemplation has found;

Meditation aspires to enjoyment, contemplation enjoys;

Meditation is a laborious effort, contemplation is a repose;

Meditation is work with fruit, contemplation is fruit without labor;

Meditation reasons, contemplation sees intuitively;

Meditation and the prayer of simplicity are an abstract knowledge, contemplation is a concrete and experimental knowledge;

Meditation makes us think of the divine friend, Contemplation makes us feel him present and acting;

Meditation and a prayer of simplicity are the fruits of our industry, Contemplation is passive; it is a gift of God that operates in us and without our help, if we are docile.

Aquinas Three Modes of Contemplation

According to Aquinas there are three modes by which it is possible to contemplate God[110] First, in his essence without any psychological medium of impressed and expressed species: quoting St. Augustine, he calls this "noon knowledge": God's knowledge of himself, sometimes shared with angels and the blessed.

Second, by the action of impressed species infused supernaturally on the mind – so called "morning knowledge": a grace granted gratuitously.

Third, by the reflection of creative things and in abstract concepts, in which we contemplate the first cause through its effects. This is "evening knowledge" – common to all men and all fallen angles, according to their respective natures.

The second mode is what concerns us. St. Teresa says of this knowledge:

So, in the beginning, when I attained to some degree of

supernatural prayer – I speak of the prayer of quiet,"[111]… "I thought I had a sense of the presence of God; this was true, and I can try to be in the state of recollection before him. God will have the soul comprehend that his Majesty is so near to it. Our Emperor and Lord will have us know that he understands us; and also have us understand what his presence brings about.[112]

This prayer is a supernatural state to which no effort of our own can raise us, because here the soul is in repose – or rather, our Lord gives it peace by his presence, as he did to the just man Simeon. Thus, all the faculties are calm, and in some manner, in no way connected with the exterior senses, the spirit realizes that it is close to God, and that if you drew but a little nearer to him, it would become one with him by union.[113]

God visits the soul in a manner that prevents its doubting, on returning to itself, that it dwelt in him and that he was within it. I know of someone who was unaware of God's being in all things by presence, power and essence, yet was firmly convinced of it by a divine favor of the sort. She asked an ill instructed priest of the kind I mentioned to tell her in what way God was within us: He answered that the Almighty was only present in us by grace. Yet so strong was her conviction of the truth learned during her prayers that she did not believe him.[114]

Saint Alphonsus Rodriguez says: "This sensation of the presence of God is not obtained by way of imagination, but there is in it a true certitude received from on high. It is a spiritual and experimental certainty that God is in the soul and in every place."[115]

St. Francis de sales: "The soul that is in quiet before God insensibly draws in the sweetness of this presence without reasoning… It possesses such a sweet vision of its Spouse present that discourse would be of no use…The soul has no need of memory in this repose, because it's Beloved is present. Nor has it any need of the imagination, for what need is there to represent by image, either exterior or interior, him in whose presence it rejoices?"[116]

None of these saints refers to visions in these citations. Rather, they allude to an obscure but sweet contact, including, at times caresses, embraces, touches, and sometimes a vision more or less luminous, either of the presence or of the nature of God – although, here we are referring to those visions that accompany higher degrees of contemplation.

St. Theresa's vision of the Blessed Trinity describes:

I see clearly that the Persons are distinct, as I saw it yesterday when you, my father, were talking to the Father Provincial; only I saw nothing, and heard nothing, as I have already told you. But there's a strange certainty about it all; the eyes of the soul see nothing. Yet when the presence is withdrawn, that withdrawal is felt…Though the Persons are distinct in a strange way, soul knows only one God.[117]

Father Alphonsus answered me that once he was transported in rapture, to which heaven he does not know, but he remembers, and can never forget. He saw the divine Essence. This vision took place with certain limitations which he was only able to explain by means of the following comparison: The divine Essence would be, so to speak, hidden by two veils (transparent) which needed to be withdrawn in order that it might be seen. He saw it only imperfectly, because only one veil was removed; but those that are in glory, that is, the blessed, see it without the veils and therefore perfectly.[118]

St. Thomas Aquinas experienced the same phenomenon:

> It is not by knowledge, but by ignorance, with the aid of a certain supernatural union with divine things, that the contemplative knows God…, And in this state of knowledge he is directly illumined by the very depths of the divine and inscrutable Wisdom."[119] "Yes, even in this life, when the eye of the soul has been purified by the gift of understanding, God can be seen after a certain fashion.[120]

Cardinal Bona reports from his own experience:

> In its higher degrees, contemplation is a sweet, calm and lovable vision of the eternal Truth, which the mind perceives by a pure glance, without multiplicity of reasonings, and which it penetrates with the great love and equally great admiration, with so much certitude and clearness that it is raised to the face-to-face intuition of God; not, however, to the extent of the glory of the blessed, but in a lesser light, still obscure based on faith, in which it finds its perfection and great enlightenment.[121]

There is nothing, then, opposed to the fact of the vision of the divine Essence being granted on earth, by exception and in very rare cases, to privileged saints, at least when they are in the ecstatic state and have completely lost the use of their corporal senses. The only words St. Catherine of Siena could utter after her experience of mystical marriage: *vidi arcana Dei* ("I saw the mysteries of God").

There is, nonetheless, an intermediate stage between infused or mystical contemplation, as above described, and ordinary or ascetic prayer. In the same way that in the visible universe the changes of nature are never abrupt (*natura non facit saltum*), that is, the lowest degrees of the higher species (Although remaining specifically distinct) are closely related to the highest degree of the lower species. So too, we see something similar in the supernatural order.

In this case it would be the highest degree of the prayer of simplicity that would border upon the lowest degree of the part of quiet. But if it be granted that sometimes they are indiscernible to the eye of man, yet nonetheless the eye of God sees not only appearances, but peers into the things themselves. But there will always be an essential difference between knowledge through infused species and knowledge without infused species; between prayer in which there is a consciousness of the real presence of God and his action within us, and prayer in which this consciousness is wanting; between the contemplation that ends in the presence of the divine reality and one that ends only in its abstract idea or in its image; between a passive state in which "God does all" as St. Theresa says, and that which is the fruit of our activity, of our own efforts aided by the ordinary help of grace. Here we have four radical differences that are of kind, not of degree.

Further Objects of the Infused Prayer of Contemplation

Beyond the obscure vision of the divine essence, saints report having visions of the mysteries of Christ's life death, passion, resurrection, heaven, purgatory, the Blessed Virgin Mary, saints, angels, demons, etc.

Efficient Causes of the Infused Prayer of Contemplation

Remote preparation: In the first place, purity of heart, by which is meant freedom from faults and imperfections intentionally committed. According to the formal teaching of sacred Scripture, only those whose hearts are perfectly pure are admitted to the contemplation of God: *Blessed are the pure of heart for they shall see God*

(Mt 5:8). But so complete a purity of heart is not obtained without the habitual practice of the virtue; above all, of perfect charity and of active or habitual union with God, which is the ordinary forerunner of a more perfect and exalted passive union.

In order that God may make himself heard or show himself, he demands silence, calm, and relief from all outward turmoil (*cfr* Hosea 2:14).

Approximate preparation: The soul can also cooperate by proximate dispositions. It often happens that during ordinary prayer, it finds itself suddenly raised to the higher-level. The truth, considered and reflected upon in discursive meditation, becomes suddenly so intimate, through the enlightenment of grace, that the soul suspends all discursive labor and allows itself to be absorbed by a sense of admiration and love. In this case, we are still dealing with the fruit of prayer in the ordinary way.

There are holy souls who will never be admitted to the higher forms of contemplation, regardless of how great their merit and sanctity. Why is this? Teresa replies, "God alone knows."

Signs that a Privileged Soul has the Vocation to be a Contemplative according to St John of the Cross[122]

The first is the recognition that the soul can no longer meditate or make use of the imagination to think of God; while able to use it freely with regard to profane things. This difficulty, however, or impotence of the mind to reason and to use the imagination, might come, not from an essential incapacity, but from the simple negligence of the soul which has developed the unfortunate the habit of allowing itself to fall into constant distractions during meditation. We must therefore supplement it with the second sign.

The second sign is an awareness of a disinclination to fix the imagination or sense faculties on other particular objects, exterior or interior. This does not mean that the imagination will cease to come and go – for even in deep recollection it usually wanders freely – but the person does not want to fix purposely on extraneous things.[123]

A third sign, and this is the surest, must therefore be added: a person likes to remain alone in loving awareness of God, without particular considerations, interior peace and quiet and repose, and without the acts and exercises (at least discursive, those in which one progresses from point-to-point) of the intellect, memory and will. Such a one prefers to remain only in the general loving awareness and knowledge he mentioned, without any particular knowledge or understanding.

In order to abandon the state of meditation safely and enter that contemplation and spirit, spiritual persons must observe within themselves all of these three signs together. The united presence of these three signs is, according to St. John of the Cross, decisive, and is evidence of the existence of a true vocation to the contemplative life.

The Act of Contemplation

The process passes through two successive phases, as in the case of all of their feelings. The former, that of passivity properly so called under the action of God which lays hold of us, is purely passive and, in itself, in no way meritorious on our part: just as we have no merit in being rained upon or the warmth produced by a fire. It merely happens to us. It is not a vital act on our part, but a vital passion, and merit is only to be found in free acts, and not in passively received impressions.

The second phase, on the other hand, is that of vital reactions. Firstly, that of the intelligence, which season contemplates; this vital act would not be free or meritorious without the consent of the will, which alone is able to be free and to merit, through its acts of acquiescence, complacence, love, recognition, etc.… As a result, even the beatific vision of heaven, although it is a vital act, is yet neither free nor meritorious.

St. Teresa and St. John of the Cross explains this important distinction of the two phases. First, from St. Teresa:

> With the assistance of God's grace we can help ourselves to a certain extent in these two matters: not so in contemplation; that is beyond our natural powers, and God does all, for it is his work. We can take no active part in this work…The soul does no more than wax which receives the impression of the seal…[124]

And from St. John of the Cross:

> in this loving awareness the soul receives God's self-communication passively, just as people receive light passively without doing anything else but keeping our eyes open. This reception of the light infused to supernaturally into the soul is passive knowing. It is affirmed that these individuals do nothing, not because they failed to understand but because they understand with no effort other than receiving what is bestowed. This is what happens when God bestows illumination and inspirations, although here the person feeling receives this general obscure knowledge.[125]

To contemplate is to receive.

In all the good actions which are produced through the ordinary inspiration of the Holy Spirit – such as the case in the act of faith – the act is completely of God as first cause, and completely of man as a secondary cause, and all the while there is one sole act, wherein it is impossible to distinguish two successive and chronologically distinct phases. In the sensation of the divine, on the other hand, there are two phases, or, if the expression be preferred, two actions of grace. The former is operating in us and without our help and produces a passive involuntary state of which we are conscious. The second operates in us and with our aid and produces voluntary and meritorious vital reactions.

In the former, it is God who does all, and man, incapable of cooperating in divine action that surpasses his powers, must be content to simply let God act. Passivity under the mystic touch and the non-mystical passivity, then are not the same thing. In the latter case it is partial only; in the former total: it is a borderline case, like that of a circle relative to a polygon inscribed within it, whose sides, if multiplied infinitely in number, draw continually closer to the circle without ever equaling it. These are two different species; or better, two different worlds.

Mystical contemplation is completely passive beneath the hand of God; its role of activity or of cooperation is reduced to consenting. In the ordinary way it should have distantly prepared itself for this, negatively by the purification of the senses, and positively by the acquisition of the virtue; and yet this preparation is not absolutely required, as God, by his power, is able to bring about good from deficiency in an instant. Hence, St. Teresa's famous phrase, "God does all." Thomas agrees. He says: the whole work belongs to grace alone.

Effects of Mystical Contemplation

These effects may be divided into groups of a very different nature. First, those that are passing, like the act of contemplation itself; and then those that are permanent and remain after it.

The passing effects are inseparable from the act of contemplation; they are rather constituent elements of that act, and therefore cease with it. The following may be considered as the principle effect.

The first is the passive and involuntary recollection of the powers of the soul, described by St Teresa as the antechamber of quiet for the first degree of infused contemplation. As soon as it is granted, a more or less complete suspension or ligature of the powers ensues. Firstly, in the understanding, which is not inactive, but can no longer act according to its usual manner. The discourse of power of the reasoning is bound, and the intuitive power exerts itself upon new objects, such as the presence of God. Little by little, all the other faculties become bound, even to the organs of sense, which in ecstasy become insensible and immovable, and we shall explain further along.

The second effect is the wonder that immediately follows the suspending exaltation of the mind. This wonder may proceed from two causes: either the suddenness and novelty of the vision infused into the soul for contemplation, or the very nature of the object, the sublimity or depth of which surpasses the powers of the intellect and confounds the understanding.

The third effect, the intellectual the sense of wonder must be added the light of the heart, *love*, which all mystics, without exception, declared to be inseparable from contemplation.

The Permanent Effects of Contemplation

The first permanent effect of contemplation is peace of the soul. The second is the ever-increasing tenderness of conscience. The third effect is a profound humility, with its companion obedience.

The fourth effect is the gift of fortitude. Contemplation finds its end in love, a love, indeed, as far beyond the ordinary as is the light of contemplation itself. The soul reaches to the point where it defies every creature in heaven and earth and even death itself, rather than break the tenacious knot of divine charity: "Who then shall separate us from the love of Christ? Tribulation? or distress? or famine? or nakedness? or danger? or persecution? or the sword? But in all these things we overcome because of him that has loved us...No creature shall separate from the love of God, which is in Jesus Christ."[126]

The fifth effect is hunger and thirst for justice. And the sixth is longing for heaven and increasing contempt for all else.

Duration of Contemplation

Contemplation is relatively short. Aquinas says:

Doubtless there is no intrinsic contradiction in the idea of and uninterrupted and endless act of contemplation. Such is the contemplation of the blessed in heaven. But, on earth, this appears to be contrary to the laws that govern the union of the soul and the body. First of all, no operation of the mind is perpetual, and all are subject to the suspensions and relaxations required by organic life, such as rest and sleep. If such is the case with every human act in this mortal life, all the more must be so in the case of the most intense and sublime act of all, for it is the culminating point of the spiritual life.[127]

St. Teresa says: "The prayer of union: the first lasted but a short time; I know not how long but perhaps for the space of an Ave Maria. I do not think I have ever been in rapture for longer than a half an hour."[128] Of course there are exceptions in the lives of the saints. St. Francis was enraptured for hours on end. He was an exception.

We may conclude from these helpful principles, coming to us from the most authoritative witnesses and masters of the spiritual life, that we must distrust it if the phenomenon of contemplation appears to continue for too long a time. It might be easily confused with that which precedes or follows it; above all one might easily mistake it for infused contemplation of a very much lower and more usual kind of prayer which, while supernatural, is not extraordinary. Further, the evil one can easily imitate such states, albeit with other idiosyncrasies, in order to derail a would-be saint.

-5-

General Guiding Principles Regarding Accidental Extraordinary Mystical Phenomena

If we are treating diabolical interventions in the order of counterfeit extraordinary mystical phenomena, then we must first grasp what authentic extraordinary mystical phenomena looks like.

Essential extraordinary mystical phenomenon is precisely that – essential. On the other hand, accidental extraordinary phenomena, as such, are not a necessary aspect of the mystical life. In other words, accidental extraordinary mystical phenomena found throughout the Church's history can only be taken seriously if the essential grace of infused contemplation has been granted. Such accidental phenomena can take numerous forms, which are described below.

Visions: corporeal, imaginative, and intellectual—to be studied with more detail later.

Locutions: auricular, imaginative, and intellectual—to be studied with more detail later.

Ecstasy: Suspension of the exterior senses and immersion in the Beloved. St. Catherine of Siena and many other saints are examples of this.

Levitation: Ascensional ecstasy: the body is raised from the ground without any natural support. St. Dominic Savio and St. Thomas Aquinas are examples of this; ecstatic flight: their bodies fly to great heights in balance themselves. St. Joseph of Cupertino is an example of this; ecstatic progress: they skimmed the ground or the water rapidly, close to earth but not touching the ground. St. Paulinus of Nola is an example of this.

Stigmata: wounds similar to those of Christ, spontaneously appearing in the body, not obeying the laws of nature with regard to healing. St. Francis of Assis, St. Pio of Pietralcina, are examples of this.

Luminous effluvia: Halos and light emanating from the body. St. Sharbel is an example of this.

Fragrant effluvia: Delightful aromas such as that of roses coming from the body. St. Dominic Guzman is an example of this.

Gift of tears: Accompanying contemplation, gentle and without distress. St. Ignatius of Loyola is an example of this.

*Supernatural abstinence***:** Prolonged fasting and only consuming the Eucharist – sometimes over the course of years. St. Catherine of Siena and, more recently, Martha Robin are examples of this.

Empire over creatures: authority over wild animals and demons. St. Francis of Assisi, St. Anthony of Padua, and St. John of the Cross are examples of this.

Glossolalia: The ability to speak one's own language and be understood in other languages. The Apostles at Pentecost are an example of this; the ability to speak the language of one's hearer's at the same linguistic level of one's own mother tongue. St. Vincent

Ferrer is an example of this.

Not all mystics have experienced all or, indeed, any of the above mentioned accidental mystical phenomena, but anyone who has authentically experienced them is a mystic. The devil can replicate most of them (he and his dupes run into difficulties when attempting supernatural abstinence, though). Yet such diabolical counterfeits are doubtful in cases where the essential mystical grace can be confirmed.

Since St. John of the Cross only deals with visions and locutions, we will treat these phenomena exclusively. First, some general considerations and foundational concepts regarding these extraordinary phenomena.

Visions

Corporeal (external) Visions: this kind of vision is the perception of some naturally invisible external object, by means of the natural organ of sight. In this case, the marvel consists in the actual apparition of the object, and not in its perception, which takes place in accordance with the normal use of sight.

For example, the apparition of Jesus Christ risen from the dead to the Apostles gathered in the cenacle: *see my hands and feet, that is I myself; Touch and see, for a spirit has no flesh and bones as you see I have.* No extraordinary phenomena occurred in the souls of the Apostles that afforded them this vision – they simply used their natural senses to see and hear our Lord who appeared in an extraordinary fashion.

To qualify as an external vision, it is not necessary that the object of the vision be of flesh and bones, simply, that it is sensible or visible by the natural organ. In this case external vision is a more solicitous term than corporeal vision.

Of the three types of supernatural vision, this is the least sublime in St. John's estimation. Although St. John considers that God desires to perfect our sense life by such supernatural gifts, provided we are ready for them (few are in this life), our Lord usually prefers to communicate directly with the soul. He also adds that these phenomena are often of demonic origin, as we shall see later. In other words, the more exterior of the experience, the less certain it is to be a divine origin. An important principle to keep in mind is that nothing of the senses can unite us to God, since it bears no proportion to God himself.

Imaginative Visions: Mystics define it as a sensible representation, produced, either when awake or asleep, in the imagination by God. They also state that imaginative visions are by far the most numerous in the lives of the saints. Thomas Aquinas says:

> Both a good and a bad angel by their own natural power can move the human imagination This may be explained as follows. For it was already stated that corporeal nature obeys the angel as regards local movement, so that whatever can be caused by the local movement of bodies is subject to the natural power of the angels. Now it is manifest that imaginative apparitions are sometimes caused in us by the local movement of animal spirits and humors… Indeed, the commotion of the spirits and humors may be so great that such appearances may even occur to those who are awake, as is seen in mad people, and the like. So, as this happens by a natural disturbance of the humors, and sometimes also by the will of man who voluntarily imagines what he previously experienced, so also the same may be done by the power of a good or a bad angel sometimes with alienation from the bodily senses, sometimes without such alienation.[129]

Therefore, even outside the domain of possession or obsession, the devil may trouble or excite the imagination. He goes on to say,

"An angel changes the imagination, not indeed by the impression of an imaginative form in no way previously received from the senses (for he cannot make a man born blind imagine color), but by local movement of the spirits and moods."[130]

According to St. John of the Cross, imaginary visions are at a higher level than corporeal visions. God works immediately upon the internal senses, so can the devil. John mentions visions of this sort, that is, visions that occur entirely within the mind, are more common than those occurring through the means of the external senses. And just as corporeal visions, so too, imaginative visions are to be rejected.

The following Teresian quotes in this section provide us with some details regarding imaginative visions. Where not otherwise indicated, they are taken from her *Interior castles,* 6th Mansions, chapter 8 and *Life* chapter 28 ff.

Object: "When our Lord is pleased to caress the soul, he allows it to envision his most Sacred Humanity, under whatever form he chooses; either as he was during his life on earth, or after his resurrection."

Time of Occurrence (during our outside of ecstasy – always unexpected):

Sometimes it is outside the time of ecstasy, and (the visions) are quite unexpected. Sometimes a person is not thinking of seeing anything, nor has any such idea crossed his mind, when suddenly the vision is revealed in its entirety, causing within the powers and senses of the soul a fright and confusion which soon afterwards become blissful peace."

At other times the imaginative vision occurs during the ecstasy or even produces it.

The former vision, which, as I said, represented God without any likeness of him, it is of a higher kind… these two visions come almost always together, and they do so come; for we behold the exigency and beauty and glory of the most Sacred Humanity with the eyes of the soul. And in the other way – that of intellectual vision (more about that later) – we learn how he as God Almighty, can do all things, commands all things, governs all things.

So exceedingly great is the power of this vision, when our Lord reveals to the soul his grandeur and majesty, that it is impossible, in my opinion, for any soul to endure it, if our Lord did not help him in a most supernatural way, by throwing it into a trance or ecstasy whereby the vision of the Divine presence is lost in the fruition there of.

If the imaginative vision occurs when there is no ecstasy, does it always produce it? Simply put, no. One of these phenomenon does not necessarily effect the other – although, as we have seen, St. Teresa says it can happen. St. John of the Cross speaks of these visions: "that supernatural light, wherein he beholds what God wills, most easily most distinctly, whether they be things of Heaven or earth; neither is there presence nor their absence an impediment to the vision.[131]

Reality of These Visions:

> Now and then it seems to me that what I saw was an image; but most frequently it was not so. I thought it was Christ himself, judging by the brightness in which he was pleased to show himself. Sometimes the vision was so indistinct, but I thought it was an image, but still not like a picture, however

well painted… If what I saw was not an image, it was a living image – not made, but the living Christ: risen from the dead… no one can have any doubt that it is our Lord himself, especially after Communion: we know that he is then present, for faith says so."

Duration: "The vision of him passed so quickly that it may be compared to a flash of lightning."

"When anyone can contemplate the sight of our Lord for a long time, I do not believe it is a vision, rather some self-suggested idea."

"God puts it before us so instantaneously, that we could not open our eyes in time to see it, if it were necessary for us to open them at all. But whether our eyes be open or not it makes little difference whatsoever."

St. John of the Cross says the same thing:

When these visions occur, it is as if a door opened into a marvelous light, whereby the soul sees, as men do, when the lightning suddenly flashes in the dark of night. The lightning makes the surrounding objects visible for an instant. And then leaves them in obscurity, both forms of them remaining in the imagination.

Great beauty:

"These visions possess great beauty and perfection. So beautiful are glorified bodies, that the glory that surrounds them renders those who see that which is so super natural and beautiful beside themselves... If I were to spend many years in devising how to picture myself anything so beautiful, I would never be able, nor even know-how to do it; for it is beyond the reach of any possible imagination here below: the whiteness and brilliancy alone are inconceivable."

Note the vividness of provisions contrasts with the difficulty that she had in her ordinary state and picturing our Lord to herself.

"As to the visions of which I am speaking, there are no means of bringing them about; ...And there is no possibility of taking anything away from it or adding anything to it; nor is there any way of bringing it about, no matter what we may do. Trying to gaze upon it – part of the vision in particular – the vision of Christ was lost at once... I was extremely desirous to behold the color of his eyes, so that I might be able to describe them, yet I never attained to the sight of them, and I could do nothing for that end; on the contrary, I lost the vision altogether."

In the imaginative vision "it is no more possible to continue looking at it, than to gaze for a long time on the sun."

Certainty:

The soul for some time afterwards possesses such certainty that this grace comes from God, that, whatever people may say to the contrary, it cannot fear a delusion. Later on, when her confessor suggests doubts to her, God may allow such a person to waver in her belief for a time, and to feel misgivings, lest, in punishment for sins, she may possibly have been left to go astray. However, she does not give way too these apprehensions, but - as I said in speaking of other matters - they only affect her in the same way as the temptations of the devil against faith, which may disturb the mind, but do not shake the firmness of belief. In fact, the more the evil one assails her with fears, the more certain does she feel that she could never have produced the great benefits she is conscious of having received, because he exercises no such power over the interior of the soul. He may present a false apparition, but it does not possess the truth, operations, and efficacy of the ones she has seen.

Sentiments produced:

The Divine Master causes within the powers and senses of the soul of fright and conclusion which soon afterwards changes into a blissful peace. Thus, after St. Paul was thrown prostrate on the ground, a great tempest and noise followed from heaven; so, in the interior world of the soul, there is a violent tumult, followed instantly, as I said, perfect calm.

The soul to whom God grants his vision almost always falls into an ecstasy, nature being too weak to bear so dread the sight. I say dread, although the apparition is more lovely and delightful than anything that could be imagined, even though one lives a thousand years, and spent all that time and trying to picture, for it so far surpass the limits of our imagination and understanding; yet the presence of such surpassing majesty inspires us over the great fear.

St. John of the Cross says:

the effects which these imaginative visions in the soul produce are quiet, illumination, joy like that of glory, sweetness, purity and love, humility and the inclination or elevation of the mind to God, sometimes more, sometimes less, sometimes more of one, sometimes more of another, according to the disposition of the soul and the will of God… those of Satan result in dryness of spirit, and a tendency to self-esteem… And in no degree whatever do they produce the gentleness of humility and love of God… they are remembered… with great aridity of spirit, and without the fruit of humility and love which issue out of the good visions whenever they are recalled.[132]

Knowledge imparted: "Certain sublime truths have been so impressed upon the mind that needs no other master. Yet diabolical counterfeits in the imagination, on the other hand, have no power to increase our knowledge in this way."

Observance of propriety in the visions: "There never was any thing in any of these spiritual visitations that was not wholly pure and clean, nor do we think it can be otherwise if the spirit be good and the visitations supernatural."

On the other hand, "these Satanic visions are very different things… The joy which Satan ministers must be, I think, very different – it shows no traces of pure and holy love."

Effects on conduct: For as there were mostly persons in the place… And so my state was talked about and came to the knowledge of many… all who knew me saw clearly that my soul was changed – and so my confessor affirmed; for the difference was very great in every way. For I saw that I had become at once another person through the instrumentality of these visions.

And it is from this that it comes to pass that he in whom God works these graces – visions of our Lord – despises himself, and becomes humbler than he ever was before, for he sees that this is a gift of God, and that he can neither add to it nor take from it.

Persistence in memory: "The most glorious picture makes an impression on the imagination, and I believe it can never be erased until the soul at last sees Christ, and enjoys him forever. While, on the other hand, illusory visions pass from the memory more quickly than do dreams."

This brings us to a second very important conclusion: the images that the devil is able to produce within us never go beyond our previous knowledge or the natural scope of our mind. Hence, the importance of not seeing evil pictures and videos or hearing evil talk or music etc. In doing so, we simply hand over very personalized weapons to our enemy with which to attack us.

Intellectual Visions

The most subtle and prodigious sort of vision is of the intellectual sort. St. John of the Cross says, "they are whatever the intellect receives in a manner resembling sight."[133] The intellectual vision, then, is distinguished from other intellectual knowledge by its object, which is transcendent, at least in its mode of manifestation.

It differs from it also in its form. It is, in fact, sudden and immediate intuition without either labor, delays, or successive progress, or calculations of human knowledge. It is a knowledge received, not acquired; it is passive, like all mystical states.

Unlike St. Teresa, St. John of the Cross claims that this sort of vision can be caused by the devil and categorizes the temptations of Christ in the desert as an example of diabolical intellectual visions.

Since holiness and spiritual progress are not bound up in extraordinary, accidental mystical phenomena, St. John of the Cross says that these visions are also to be rejected. St. John of the Cross counsels us to approach our Lord in the darkness of faith, and not in the light of the extraordinary. Teresa explains:

> A person who is in no way expecting such a favor nor has ever imagined herself worthy of receiving it, is conscious that Jesus Christ stands by her side, although she sees neither with the eyes of the body nor of the soul (the imagination). This is called an intellectual vision; I cannot tell why at first it distressed her, for she could not understand it; she could see nothing yet so convinced did she feel that Jesus Christ was thus in some way manifesting himself that she could not doubt that it was some kind of vision... She was alarmed, never having heard of an intellectual vision. This presence is quite evident and certain, and indeed, far more so than the ordinary presence of other people about which we may be deceived; but such is not so the case here.

She continues:

> this vision, that is the intellectual vision, unlike an imaginary one, does not pass away quickly, but lasts for several days, and even sometimes for year... A most tender love for him results from being constantly in his company... Or makes the soul conscious that he is close at hand.

It is distinguishable by its effects, and this is the practical test on which it is impossible to insist too much. The first and most remarkable of these effects is a greatly increasing humility. "This favor brings with it an overwhelming sense of self abasement and humility; the reverse will be the case if it came from Satan." She goes on to say, "although I believe some of the former favors are more sublime, yet this brings with it a special knowledge of God." The greater the divine light of God's infinite majesty and holiness is revealed, the greater our conviction of our misery and our nothingness.

"It brings with it graces and special effects which could not possibly come from melancholy. Nor could the devil thus fill the soul with such peace, with a constant desire to please God, and such utter contempt of all that does not lead to him."

In accordance with the principles which we have already laid down, and in agreement with St. Thomas, God alone is able to act directly on the mind and to enlighten it; the devil can only act on it through the medium of the senses, whether internal or external. Now, it is precisely the property of this vision to contain nothing sensible and is incapable of being induced or disturbed by the senses. Therefore, it is outside the grasp of the devil and escapes his deceit. In order to deceive us, the devil would be reduced to provoking imaginative visions we might mistake for intellectual; but the snare is too clumsy for an attentive soul schooled in their distinctions.

St. Teresa says:

it seems to me that this is the state with which the devil can least interfere… The vision and the language (involved) are matters of such pure spirituality, that there is no turmoil of the faculties, or of the senses, from which… the devil can derive any advantage.

Another reason St. Teresa calls to mind, for she had already repeated it several times, is that it is only in the second period of the ecstasy that the soul hears divine locutions and receives visions. In the first, all the powers of the soul are wholly lost in God, and it can neither see, nor understand, nor hear anything else. God becomes its absolute master. Therefore, there is no longer room for the devil, nor even for the wanderings of our imagination.

Hence the absolute certitude which pervades a soul after having experienced the divine vision. It can no longer doubt what it has seen and heard: "our Lord wills that this knowledge be so graven on the understanding that we can no more question his presence than that which we see with our eyes."

Finally, there is left an effect or pledge of this vision in the soul thus favored which remains there as a continual witness of its divine truth, which St. Teresa calls infused knowledge. "Even that little, which is nothing more than the bare active listening, which is granted to it in the other case, is now out of its power. It finds its food prepared and eaten; there is nothing more to do except to enjoy. It is as if one, without ever learning, without taking the pains even to learn to read, and without studying any subject whatever, were to find oneself in possession of all knowledge, not knowing how or why it came to him, seeing that he has never taken the trouble to learn the alphabet… The soul finds itself learned in a moment, and the mystery of the Most Holy Trinity so clearly revealed to it, together with other most profound doctrines, that there is no theologian in the world with whom it would hesitate to dispute for the truth of these matters."

Description and Object of Intellectual Visions according to St. Teresa

She sees nothing either outwardly or inwardly… But without seeing anything, she understands what it is, and where it is, more clearly than if she saw it, only nothing in particular presents itself to her. She is like a person who feels that another is close beside her; but because she is in the dark she sees nothing… Without a word, inward or outward, also clearly perceives who it is, where he is and occasionally what he means. Why or how she perceives it, she knows not; so it is.

"her confessor... Asked her how, if she saw nothing, she knew that our Lord was near, and had her describe his appearance. She said she was unable to, for she cannot see his face, nor could she tell more than she already said, but that she was sure she was right, and that it was he who spoke to her... You may ask: if we see no one, how can we know whether it is Christ, or is most glorious Mother, or a saint.? One cannot answer this question, or know how one distinguishes them, but the fact remains undoubted."

"Jesus Christ seems to be by my side continually, and this vision was not imaginary, for I saw no form...It is very rarely that I saw Satan assume a bodily form; I know of his presence through the vision I have spoken of before, the vision wherein no form is seen."

Alvarez de Paz says that,

Intellectual visions are sometimes very distinct, and others, on the contrary, are confused. If we see Jesus Christ or the Blessed Virgin in the second manner, we see nothing formed, with regard either to the face or the body, and yet we know more certainly than by the evidence of the eyes... It is as though you were suddenly, in the darkness, to feel that someone is beside you, and to know that benevolence - not enmity - is felt towards you; but you are quite ignorant as to whether it is a man or woman, young or old, good-looking or no, and whether standing or sitting. Perhaps you would like to know whether we see the person who appears thus intellectually, as he really is? I reply that, with regard to the angels, they show themselves present really and by their substance. As for our Lord's Body, in order to be seen close to us intellectually, there is no need for him to leave heaven, for a sound philosophy teaches us that God can come in the absence of an object, represent it to us just as it would appear if it were present.[134]

-6-

John of the Cross' Treatment of Diabolical Counterfeit Visions and Locutions

When St. John of the Cross writes about the spiritual and mystical life, he adheres to the principles of the interpretation of Scripture laid down by St. Thomas. He makes use of the spiritual sense of the words of Scripture in a very edifying manner, without falling into sentimental extravagances common to his epoch.

In chapter 19 of the Book II of *The Ascent of Mount Carmel*, in which he deals with the issue of deception in the context of authentic visions and locutions, he mentions that this is on account of two reasons: First, "the defective way in which we understand them," and second, "…and the other, the variety of their causes."

He goes on to illustrate from Sacred Scripture how many prophesies and words of God were not fulfilled as expected because men "understood them after their own manner… very literally," whereas "the principal intention of God in giving these things is to express and convey the spirit which is in them… (which) is much more pregnant in meaning than the letter, and is very extraordinary, and goes far beyond its limits." Among other examples he points to those prophecies relating to our Lord Jesus Christ, which the many Jews of Jesus' day missed, since they took them in the strict sense, the fact being "that these prophecies have been understood, concerning Christ, spiritually, in which since they were entirely true."

Easy Marks for Satan

If well-intentioned, good people can misunderstand the content of authentic public and private revelations, how much room there must be for people of mixed intentions to be led astray? Amongst these are the spiritually sensual, i.e., people who long for consolations. But also the spiritually proud, that is, those people who consider themselves specially favored by our Lord, those who long to stand out, those who are not satisfied with the ordinary path of holiness which presents enough hurdles in itself. Further, John says that people who are prone to see the sensational where it is not are especially prey to this demonic device. He says:

> In this type of locution -- namely, in successive interior words -- the devil frequently intervenes, especially in the case of such as have some inclination or affection for them. At times when such persons begin to be recollected, the devil is accustomed to offer them ample material for distractions, forming conceptions or words by suggestion in their understanding, and then corrupting and deceiving it most subtly with things that have every appearance of being true.[135]

Senses and Simulated Visions

"To these people the devil will often simulate visions and other

73

experiences so as to keep them in his service."[136]

At the other extreme we find St. John's treatment of demonic activity in the life of contemplative souls. Given the inestimable and, nonetheless, hidden good these people bring about for the entire Mystical Body, Satan has a particular fear of and, therefore, interest in their prayer lives. He exhausts his resources with them.

It is very revealing how much attention and energy the Evil One spends on prayerful people, attempting to distract them from their salvific work. Although the devil cannot see the work of grace in a soul, he is privy to some of its effects – and it frightens him to no end.

St. John of the Cross tells us that the Evil One will dedicate more attention and energy to disturbing the prayer of a contemplative than on many people who do not pray:

The devil considers this so important that it is worth noting that, since he accomplishes more through a little harm caused in these souls than by great damage effected in many others, as we have mentioned, there is hardly anyone walking this path on whom he does not bring serious harm and loss. This evil one establishes himself cautiously at the passageway from sense to spirit, deceiving souls and feeding the sensory part itself, as we said, with sensible things. The soul does not think there is any loss in this; it thus fails to enter into the inner dwelling of the Bridegroom and remains at the threshold to watch what is happening outside in the sensory part. *The devil sees every high thing,* says Job (41:25), that is, every spiritual height of souls in order to combat them. If, by chance, some soul enters a sublime recollection in such fashion that the devil cannot distract it in the way we mentioned, he struggles through horrors, fears, bodily pains, or exterior sounds and noises to make it at least advert to sense and to draw it out thereby and divert it from the interior spirit, until being able to do no more he leaves it.

But it is so easy for him to thwart and block the riches of these precious souls that even though he values doing this more than he does ruining many other souls, he still does not esteem it highly because of the ease in which he accomplishes it and the little it costs him.[137]

Other Senses and Feelings[138]

And, besides all this, when the soul sees that such extraordinary things happen to it, it is often visited, insidiously and secretly by a certain complacency, so that it thinks itself to be of some importance in the eyes of God; which is contrary to humility.

The devil, too, knows how to insinuate into the soul a secret satisfaction with itself, which at times becomes very evident; wherefore he frequently represents these objects to the senses, setting before the eyes figures of saints and most beauteous lights; and before the ears words very much dissembled; and representing also sweetest perfumes, delicious tastes and things delectable to the touch; to the end that, by producing desires for such things, he may lead the soul into much evil.

And likewise, those that come from the devil (without the consent of the soul) cause it disturbance or aridity or vanity or presumption in the spirit. Yet these are not so effective to work evil as are those of God to work good; for those of the devil can only set in action the first movements of the will, and move it no farther, unless the soul be consenting thereto; and such trouble continues not long unless the soul's lack of courage and prudence be the occasion of its continuance.

These representations and feelings, therefore, must always be rejected; for, even though some of them be of God, He is not offended by their rejection, nor is the effect and fruit which He desires to produce in the soul by means of them any the less surely received because the soul rejects them and desires them not.

The reason for this is that corporeal vision or feeling in respect to any of the other senses, or any other communication of the most interior kind, if it be of God, produces its effect upon the spirit at the very moment when it appears or is felt, without giving the soul time or opportunity to deliberate whether it will accept or reject it.

Are We to Reject Authentic Visions, too?

For, even as God gives these things supernaturally, without effort on the part of the soul, and independently of its capacity, even so likewise, without respect to its effort or capacity, God produces in it the effect that He desires by means of such things; for this is a thing that is wrought and brought to pass in the spirit passively; and thus its acceptance or non-acceptance consists not in the acceptance or the rejection of it by the will.

Do We Spurn God's Grace by Rejecting Visions?

It is as though fire were applied to a person's naked body: it would matter little whether or not he wished to be burned; the fire would of necessity accomplish its work. So too is it with visions and representations that are good: even though the soul desire it not, they work their effect upon it, chiefly and especially in the soul, rather than in the body.

But the visions that are of God penetrate the soul and move the will to love, and produce their effect, which the soul cannot resist even though it would, any more than the window can resist the sun's rays when they strike.

Although God may choose to grant extraordinary graces to certain people in this way, St. John of the Cross counsels us not to seek them, even in the case that such extraordinary phenomena were from God. To not heed his advice sets oneself up for all sorts of spiritual difficulties. Our guide identifies six of them for us.[139]

A weakening of faith: The first is that faith gradually diminishes; for things that are experienced by the senses derogate from faith; since faith, as we have said, transcends every sense. And thus, the soul withdraws itself from the means of union with God when it closes not its eyes to all these things of sense.

The Soul's atrophy is the price of the senses: Secondly, if they are not rejected, they are a hindrance to the spirit, for the soul rests in them and its spirit soars not to the invisible. This was one of the reasons why the Lord said to His disciples that it was needful for Him to go away that the Holy Spirit might come; so, too, He forbade Mary Magdalene to touch His feet, after His resurrection, that she might be grounded in faith.

Unhealthy attachments: Thirdly, the soul becomes attached to these things and advances not to true resignation and detachment of spirit.

False priorities: Fourthly, it begins to lose the effect of them and the inward spirituality which they cause, because it sets its eyes upon their sensual aspect, which is the least important. And thus, it receives not so fully the spirituality which they cause, which is impressed and preserved more securely when all things of sense are rejected, since these are very different from pure spirit.

Unintentional and unconscious rejection of God's grace: Fifthly, the soul begins to lose the favors of God, because it accepts them as though they belonged to it and profits not by them as it should. And to accept them in this way and not to profit by them is to seek after them; but God gives them not that the soul may seek after them; nor should the soul take upon itself to believe that they are of God.

Endangerment of the soul: Sixthly, a readiness to accept them opens the door to the devil that he may deceive the soul by other things like to them, which he very well knows how to dissimulate and disguise, so that they may appear to be good; for, as the Apostle says, he can transform himself into an angel of light. Of this we shall treat hereafter, by the Divine favor, in our third book, in the chapter upon spiritual gluttony.

It is always well, then, that the soul should reject these things, and close its eyes to them, regardless of their provenance. For, unless it does so, it will prepare the way for those things that come from the devil, and will give him such influence that, not only will his visions come in place of God's, but his visions will begin to increase, and those of God to cease, in such manner that the devil will have all the power and God will have none.

The Return to God Becomes Less Likely

So, it has happened to many incautious and ignorant souls, who rely on these things to such an extent that many of them have found it hard to return to God in purity of faith; and many have been unable to return, so securely has the devil rooted himself in them; for which reason it is well to resist and reject them all.

For, by the rejection of evil visions, the errors of the devil are avoided, and by the rejection of good visions no hindrance is offered to faith and the spirit harvests the fruit of them. And just as, when the soul allows them entrance, God begins to withhold them because the soul is becoming attached to them and is not profiting by them as it should, while the devil insinuates and increases his own visions, where he finds occasion and cause for them; just so, when the soul is resigned, or even averse to them, the devil begins to desist, since he sees that he is working it no harm; and contrariwise God begins to increase and magnify His favors in a soul that is so humble and detached, making it ruler over many things, even as He made the servant who was faithful in small things.

The Sin of Spiritual Lust

Beyond this, St. John tells us that in working on contemplative souls, the devil engenders disquiet, dryness, sorrow, affliction, vain and disordered pleasures.[140] He seduces them with "spiritual impurity", that subtle desire for pleasure which never even rises to the level of the senses, yet distract the soul from its recollection which should, otherwise, detach the soul from pleasures and sensible apprehensions and be fixed on the Lord (always incomprehensible), and not the self.

Divine Justice and Hidden Mercy

For sure, the devil does not lack motives to disturb us. Surprisingly, St. John of the Cross, when enumerating the reasons for diabolical involvement in our lives, points to certain "rights" the demons have over us.

God ordinarily permits the adversary to recognize favors granted through the good angels so this adversary may do what he can, in accord with the measure of justice, to hinder them. <u>Thus, the devil cannot protest his rights,</u> claiming that he is not given the opportunity to conquer the soul, as was his complaint in the story of Job (1:9-11; 2:4-5). He could do this if God did not allow a certain parity between the two warriors (the good angel and the bad) in their struggle for the soul. Hence the victory of either one will be more estimable, and the soul, victorious and faithful in temptation, will receive a more abundant reward.[141]

In other words, the evil has a degree of freedom in his range of activity and we are not without that sphere of influence. Nonetheless, the providential disposition on God's part has man's ultimate good as the divine motive. We cannot merit if we are not tested. For sure, this is a risk, but every love is a risk. The Evil One's influence of the human mind and suggestion of spiritually damaging things, testing of man in order to seduce him, is always within God's permission.

Why would God permit his children to undergo such existential trials? John offers us some convincing reasons. The most proximate are what follows.

Law of harmony: John points to what he calls "the law of harmony" and proportion which rules the universe. He explains: "We must note that this is why God permits the devil to deal with the soul in the same measure and mode in which he himself conducts and deals with it."[142] "Hence the victory of either one will be more estimable, and the soul, victorious and faithful in temptation, will receive a more abundant reward."[143] He goes on, "If a person receives true visions from the good angel, God permits the bad angel to represent false ones of the same kind. Thus, an incautious person can be deceived, as many have been."[144]

Possibility for spiritual growth: Thomas Aquinas states that the more a soul is tried by the devil the greater its reward.[145] John agrees:

> Yet it should be understood that when the good angel allows the devil the advantage of reaching the soul with this spiritual horror, he does so that it may be purified and prepared, through this spiritual vigil, for some great feast and spiritual favor that God, who never mortifies but to give life or humbles but to exalt [1 Sam. 2:6-7], desires to give. This favor will be granted a short time afterward, and the soul, in accord with the dark and horrible purgation it suffered, will enjoy a wondrous and delightful spiritual communication, at times ineffably sublime. The preceding horror of the evil spirit greatly refines the soul so it can receive this good.[146]

Divine justice meted out in time and space: So much for the benefits.

Not infrequently, such divine permission is also the result of a punishment brought upon oneself. The logical result of having entered into any sort of bond with the Evil One, so rather than effect God's mercy, such people experience the just fruits of their choices. People who venture into superstitious practices risk this: "For these are clearly evil, and involve sin, and many of them imply a secret compact with the devil; by such means these persons provoke God to wrath and not to mercy"[147]

At other times, such punishment is owed to a certain "propriety" or correspondence owing to their superstitious endeavors: And, what is worse, and indeed intolerable, is that certain persons desire to feel some effect in themselves, or to have their petitions fulfilled, or to know that the purpose of these ceremonious prayers of theirs will be accomplished.

This is nothing less than to tempt God and to anger Him greatly, so much so that He sometimes gives leave to the devil to deceive them, making them feel and understand things that are far removed from the benefit of their soul, which they deserve because of the attachment that they show in their prayers, not desiring God's will, rather than their own desires, to be done therein; and thus, because they place not their whole confidence in God, nothing goes well with them.[148]

And in this way God gives leave to the devil to blind and deceive many, when their sins and audacities merit it; and this the devil can do and does successfully, and they give him credence and believe him to be a good spirit; to such a point that, although they may be quite persuaded that he is not so, they cannot undeceive themselves, since, by the permission of God, there has already been insinuated into them the spirit of misunderstanding, even as we read was the case with the prophets of King Achab, whom God permitted to be deceived by a lying spirit, giving the devil leave to deceive them, and saying: *You shall prevail with your lie, and shalt deceive them; go forth and do so.*[149]

St. John goes on to say that the devil responds to the disordered desires that he has incited in the person, thus keeping the person in a state of deceit, believing themselves to be the object of divine visitations:

Hence necessarily follows deception by reason of his abandonment by God. And then comes the devil and makes answer according to the pleasure and desire of that man, who, being pleased thereat, since the answers and communications are according to his will, allows himself to be deceived greatly.[150] This divine retribution takes another form as a result of this pride, vanity, self-sufficiency, and rejection of the authentic things of God:

Such persons have succeeded in angering God so greatly that He has of set purpose allowed them to go astray and be deceived and to blind their own spirits and to leave the ordered paths of life and give rein to their vanities and fancies.[151]

The divine permission does not go beyond the limits of privative causality, consisting in not granting the necessary light and preservation to avoid deceit.

Angered by this, God allowed them to act foolishly, giving them no light as to that wherewith He desired not that they should concern themselves. And thus, the Prophet says that God mingled that spirit in them, privatively. And in this sense God is the cause of such an evil -- that is to say, He is the privative cause, which consists in His withdrawal of His light and favor, to such a point that they must needs fall into error.[152]

Certainly, in an age that has grown numb to the meaning of sin and believes God to be an all-merciful garden gnome, this Juanistic teaching might come as a surprise. But then so will many divine decrees on judgment day.

The Areas of Diabolical Influence

St. John compares the soul to a hill. The more visible animals on the crest of the hill are easy prey. The soul, too, has parts that are more easily visible and accessible to the Evil One, and still other aspects that remain hidden. He describes:

> To attain this divine interior exercise there is also need for solitude and withdrawal from all things presentable to the soul, whether from the lower, sensory portion, or from the higher, rational part. These two parts comprise the entire compound of human faculties and senses, and she calls this compound a "hill." All the natural knowledge and the appetites dwelling on the hill in this harmonious composite are like prey to the devil, who hunts and catches them in order to harm the soul.[153]

The devil cannot act the same way on every aspect of the soul since he is limited, not only by extrinsic norms imposed by the divine providence, but also by intrinsic restrictions derived by the nature of things: the devil's and the soul's.

John sets down this clear principle: the devil will never be able to work within the soul, at its substance but will be limited to influencing the sense areas of the soul.

It is precisely in the substance of the soul where those people who have been transformed by grace celebrate the holy nuptials with the divine Spouse. The devil has no access nor does he know exactly what the economy of grace brings about. He is blind to it and unable to reach it. John says:

> This feast takes place in the substance of the soul where neither the center of the senses nor the devil can reach. Therefore, the more interior it is, the more secure, substantial, and delightful, because the more interior it is, the purer it is. And the greater the

purity, the more abundantly, frequently, and generously God communicates himself. Thus, the delight and joy of the soul is so much more intense because God is the doer of all without the soul's doing anything. Since the soul cannot do any work of its own save through the means and aid of the corporeal senses, from which in this event it is very free and far removed, its sole occupation now is to receive from God, who alone can move the soul and do his work in its depths. Thus, all the movements of this soul are divine. Although they belong to it, they belong to it because God works them in it and with it, for it wills and consents to them.[154]

In fact, what the divine Bridegroom carries out in the depths of the soul, not even the affected individual can know or even imagine what is going on – much less the devil:

First, it calls this dark contemplation "secret" since, as we mentioned, contemplation is mystical theology, which theologians call secret wisdom and which St. Thomas says is communicated and infused into the soul through love. This communication is secret and dark to the work of the intellect and the other faculties. Insofar as these faculties do not acquire it but the Holy Spirit infuses it and puts it in order in the soul, as the bride says in the Song of Songs [Sg. 2:4], the soul neither knows nor understands how this comes to pass and thus calls it secret. Indeed, not only does the soul fail to understand, but no one understands, not even the devil, since the Master who teaches the soul dwells within it substantially where neither the devil nor the natural senses nor the intellect can reach.[155]

Beyond one's imagining, but not beyond one's awareness: as the contemplative soul develops it rapport with the Christ, it recognizes the Presence, called "substantial touches" which penetrate the substance of the soul and taste of eternity. Far from the saccharine imitations the devil hawks, the truly contemplative soul will not be deceived by cheap imitations.

The reason for this concealment is that since His Majesty dwells substantially in that part of the soul to which neither the angel nor the devil can gain access and thereby see what is happening, the enemy cannot learn of the intimate and secret communications there between the soul and God. Since the Lord grants these communications directly, they are wholly divine and sovereign. They are all substantial touches of divine union between God and the soul. In one of these touches, since this is the highest degree of prayer, the soul receives greater good than in all else.

With the correct dispositions on the part of the contemplative soul, the devil finds it very difficult, if not impossible, to successfully deceive the object of his attack.

As the soul receives this good passively, its action is at no time of any importance. Nor should it fear any deception; for neither the understanding nor the devil can intervene herein, nor can they succeed in passively producing this substantial effect in the soul, in such a way that the effect and habit of the locution may be impressed upon it, unless the soul should have given itself to the devil by a voluntary compact, and he should have dwelt in it as its master, and impressed upon it these effects, not of good, but of evil. Inasmuch as that soul would be already voluntarily united to him in perversity, the devil might easily impress upon it the effects of his sayings and words with evil intent.

For we see by experience that in many things and even upon good souls he works great violence, by means of suggestion, making his suggestions very efficacious; and if they were evil he might work in them the consummation of these suggestions. But he cannot leave upon a soul effects similar to those of locutions which are good; for there is no comparison between the locutions of the devil and those of God. [156]

"Satan can do nothing against the soul except through the soul's own powers." [157] By the soul "powers", John means the external and internal senses residing in the lower part of the soul, that part most in contact with the physical person: "Except by way of the powers of the senses, the devil could never reach the soul or know what goes on in it." [158]

On the other hand, the soul that opens itself up to diabolical influence by way of curiosity, desire for extraordinary things (special knowledge, charismatic gifts, etc.) makes itself easy prey to the devil's deceptions:

And the devil may know that a certain someone cannot in the course of nature, live more than so many years, and he may foretell this; and so with regard to many other things and in many ways that it is impossible to recount fully — nor can one even begin to recount many of them, since they are most intricate and subtle — he insinuates falsehoods; from which a soul cannot free itself save by fleeing from all revelations and visions and locutions that are supernatural.

Wherefore God is justly angered with those that receive them, for sees that it is temerity on their part to expose themselves to such great peril and presumption and curiosity, and things that spring from pride, and are the root and foundation of vainglory, and of disdain for the things of God, and the beginning of many evils to which many have come. Such persons have succeeded in angering God so greatly that He has of set purpose allowed them to go astray and be deceived and to blind their own spirits and to leave the ordered paths of life and give rein to their vanities and fancies, according to the word of Isaiah, where he says: *The Lord hath mingled in the midst thereof the spirit of dissension and confusion* (19:14). Which in our ordinary language means the spirit of misunderstanding.

What Isaiah is very plainly saying is to our purpose, for he is speaking of those who were endeavoring by supernatural means to know things that were to come to pass. And therefore, he says that God mingled in their midst the spirit of misunderstanding; not that God willed them, in fact, to have the spirit of error, or gave it to them, but that they desired to meddle with that to which by nature they could not attain. Angered by this, God allowed them to act foolishly, giving them no light as to that wherewith He desired not that they should concern themselves.

And in this way God gives leave to the devil to blind and deceive many, when their sins and audacities merit it; and this the devil can do and does successfully, and they give him credence and believe him to be a good spirit; to such a point that, although they may be quite persuaded that he is not so, they cannot undeceive themselves, since, by the permission of God, there has already been insinuated into them the spirit of misunderstanding, even as we read was the case with the prophets of King Achab, whom God permitted to be deceived by a lying spirit, giving the devil leave to deceive them, and saying: *You shall prevail with your falsehood, and shall deceive them; go forth and do so* (3 Kg 22:22).

And so well was he able to work upon the prophets and the King, in order to deceive them, that they would not believe the prophet Michah, who prophesied the truth to them, saying the exact contrary of that which the others had prophesied, and this came to pass because God permitted them to be blinded, since their affections were attached to that which they desired to happen to them, and God answered them according to their desires and wishes; and this was a most certain preparation and means for their being blinded and deceived, which God allowed of set purpose.

Thus, too, did Ezechiel prophesy in the name of God. Speaking against those who began to desire to have knowledge direct from God, from motives of curiosity, according to the vanity of their spirit, he says: When such a man comes to the prophet to enquire of Me through him, I, the Lord, will answer him by Myself, and I will set my face in anger against that man; and, as to the prophet, when he has gone astray in that which was asked of him, *I, the Lord, have deceived that prophet* (14:7). This is to be taken to mean, by not succoring him with His favor so that he might not be deceived; and this is His meaning when He says: *I the Lord will answer him by Myself in anger* (*ibid*) - that is, God will withdraw His grace and favor from that man. Hence necessarily follows deception by reason of his abandonment by God. And then comes the devil and makes answer according to the pleasure and desire of that man, who, being pleased thereat, since the answers and communications are according to his will, allows himself to be deceived greatly.[159]

With that in mind, how much more apparent is the importance of mortification of the souls' passion and powers to truncate the devil's influence. In fact, St. John says that the devil retreats in confusion, ceasing similar attacks in the face of such rebuffs.[160]

Modes of Diabolical Influence on the Human Intellect

The "how" of the devil's influence is determined by the nature of the object upon which he attempts to operate.

Through the External Senses: With regard to the external senses, he can produce present exterior objects, such as the images of saints, of beautiful scenes to one's sight; to one's auditory sense he can suggest flattering words; subtle aromas; sweet tastes; delightful touches.[161]

Feelings: He can influence us in those things concerning the worship and service of God, arousing senses joys and delights.[162]

Memories: In the sense memory the devil can insert images, ideas, and conversations with an eye to arousing pride, greed, anger, envy, etc.[163]

If the external senses seem to be off-limits in John's treatment of the diabolical suggestion, the interior senses present quite a different story. The devil has access to the memory and does not hesitate to retrieve all sorts of spiritually harmful images and recollections. St. John teaches:

> it is freed from many suggestions, temptations and motions of the devil, which he infuses into the soul by means of thoughts and ideas, causing it to fall into many impurities and sins, as David says in these words: 'They have thought and spoken wickedness.'[498] And thus, when these thoughts have been completely removed, the devil has naught wherewith to assault the soul by natural means.[164]

John says that the devil can cobble together different pieces of memory in order to present to the mind the most horrible of images.[165] With this in mind it serves us to consider the importance of guarding our exterior senses so as not to hand over weapons to the enemy to be used against us.

Imagination Piqued by Influenced External Senses: With regard to the imagination the devil is capable of suggesting images and objects, without recourse to any external sense, that the five senses apprehend by nature: yet the devil, always a master at marketing, can present them in ways even more attractive than they actually are.

Modification of That Which is Sensed Externally: It must be understood, then, that, even as the five outward senses represent the images and species of their objects to these inward senses, even so, supernaturally, as we say, without using the outward senses, both God and the devil can represent the same images and species, and much more beautiful and perfect ones.[166]

Filters: Demonic Makeover: He can even make turbid, ugly things seem sublime and beautiful. Often, in order to distract someone from prayer he can arouse impure desires. If that tactic finds a stonewall, the devil might suggest the remembrance of spiritually helpful people and things in an attempt to take one's mind off of our Lord.[167]

Just as images are of great benefit for remembering God and the saints, and for moving the will to devotion when they are used in the ordinary way, as is fitting, so they will lead to great error if, when supernatural happenings come to pass in connection with them, the soul should not be able to conduct itself as is fitting for its journey to God.

Demonic Impersonations: For one of the means by which the devil lays hold on incautious souls, with great ease, and obstructs the way of spiritual truth for them, is the use of extraordinary and supernatural happenings, of which he gives examples by means of images, both the material and corporeal images used by the Church, and also those which he is wont to fix in the fancy in relation to such or such a saint, or an image of him, transforming himself into an angel of light that he may deceive.[168]

The internal physical senses are something akin to a storehouse in which the intellect deposits and retrieves its own provisions. Both the Lord and enemy have access to that storehouse and bring their wares that are presented to the intellect.[169] This is a common area of influence for the Evil One's activity, both ordinary and extraordinary.

Not only will the devil imitate angelic communications in order to confound, appearing as an angel of light, he can also reveal himself in a non-physical way, spirit to spirit.

Not only does the devil imitate this kind of corporeal vision, but he also simulates and interferes with spiritual communications coming from a good angel, since he can discern them, as we said; and as Job said, *he beholds every sublime thing* (41:25). He imitates and interferes with them. Yet he cannot imitate and form these spiritual communications as he can those granted under some appearance or figure, for these are without form and figure, and it is of the nature of the spirit to be formless and figureless. He represents his frightful spirit to the soul in order to attack it in the same way in which it receives the spiritual communication, and to assail and destroy the spiritual with the spiritual. In this case, when the good angel communicates spiritual contemplation, the soul cannot enter the hiding place of this contemplation quickly enough to go unnoticed by the devil. He then presents himself to it with some spiritual horror and disturbance, at times very painful. Sometimes the soul can withdraw speedily without giving this horror of the evil spirit an opportunity to make an impression on it, and it recollects itself by the efficacious favor the good angel then gives it.[170]

Representations to the Intellect (intellectual images): The devil works on the intellect by way of so-called corporal visions, senses apprehensions, and imagined visions because these communications naturally correspond to the intellective faculties as their object. On the other hand, it is precisely the darkness of faith that ought to take hold of the intellect and guide it against such aberrations that derive from these apprehensions.[171]

The foundation of the Christian religion is faith. Errors and lies will be spread by demons to try to undermine this foundation. For Teresa, the devil — altogether a liar — can play many tricks, but "God will not permit him to deceive a soul which has no trust whatever in itself, and is strengthened in faith" (238).

John of the Cross is even more emphatic and advises that, for the devil, the light of faith is worse than darkness.

When the soul is clothed in faith the devil is ignorant of how to hinder it, neither is he successful in his efforts, for faith gives the soul strong protection against the devil, who is the mightiest and most astute enemy. As a result, St. Peter found no greater safeguard than faith in freeing herself from the devil, when he advised "Cui resistite fortes in fidei"(1 Pt 5:9). (Dark Night 376)'

To foster the obscurity of pure faith, the spiritual director must be careful not to foster visions, locutions, prophecies, or other kinds of extraordinary phenomena. Although these phenomena are sometimes from God, they are more often from the devil. For John of the Cross this danger was real. He understood that the devil can present to the memory many false ideas under the guise of truth, making these ideas seem so certain that the soul thinks they cannot be false, but that what it feels is in accord with truth (Ascent 227).[172]

Communications to the Intellect (ideas): Further, the evil spirit can infiltrate by purely spiritual communications - those that do not come by way of the senses, but rather in a subtler way, without actively involving the imagination.[173] Although represented after the manner of the senses, all of them are, however, received as intelligible intellect. Although the devil might be permitted to meddle with these purely spiritual communications it is not nearly quite so easy for him as it is with those that come from the senses.[174]

By way of interior words and concepts, the devil can communicate to the intellect.[175] These suggested locutions are often made of long arguments and discourses[176] or spiritual visions.[177] He can also illuminate the intellect in such a way as to impress upon it visions of corporeal things.

St. John of the Cross states that the devil hopes to convince the person under his suggestion that things simply are as he makes them appear and it cannot be any other way.[178] He says that once the suggestion has been planted, its persuasiveness will be determined, in great part, by the degree of dominion one has over his senses. As a result, prayer and self-dominion are of utmost importance in countering this demonic activity.[179]

Spiritual Visions: The devil manages to cause spiritual visions of a corporeal substance in the soul by way of intellectual concepts using the mind's natural light with which to see things even in their absence.[180]

Concepts Falsely Presented: He is also capable of subtly luring the soul by way of intellectual concepts, vividly yet falsely represented. In the case of those who are advanced along the way of configuration with Christ, they sometimes have a grasp of other people's interior that is elusive to more carnal people. John says:

But it must be known that those whose spirits are purged can learn by natural means with great readiness, and some more readily than others, that which is in the inward spirit or heart, and the inclinations and talents of men, and this by outward indications, albeit very slight ones, as words, movements and other signs.

For, even as the devil can do this, since he is spirit, even so likewise can the spiritual man, according to the words of the Apostle, who says: *He that is spiritual judgeth all things.* And again, he says: *The spirit searches all things, even, the deep things of God.*

Wherefore, although spiritual persons cannot by nature know thoughts, or things that are in the minds of others, they may well interpret them through supernatural enlightenment or by signs. And, although they may often be deceived in their interpretation of signs, they are more generally correct. Yet we must trust neither to the one means nor to the other, for the devil meddles herein greatly, and with much subtlety, as we shall afterwards say, and thus we must ever renounce such kinds of knowledge.[181]

As a result, the devil can lead a person into thinking he has a grasp of other people's inner lives, their consciences, faults, etc. in an attempt to get these advanced people to fall into calumny, sinful thought and speech so that a multitude of sins be committed through such accusations.[182]

Locutions: John tells us also that Satan is the master of private "revelations." These usually take the form of "locutions." In this kind of revelation the devil may meddle freely. For, as revelations of this nature come ordinarily through words, figures and similitudes, etc., the devil may very readily counterfeit others like them, much more so than when the revelations are in spirit alone.[183]

By way of a series of "locutions," the devil not only nudges the will to such point that it begins to desire such interior movements,[184] but he can bring about a sort of "fervor," born of disordered self-love, which leaves the souls arid and cold before the love of God.[185]

Discerning Interiorly Suggested Locutions

From what has been said, it is evident that these successive locutions may proceed in the understanding from three causes, namely: from the Divine Spirit, Who moves and illumines the understanding; from the natural illumination of the same understanding; and from the devil, who may speak to the soul by suggestion.

To describe now the signs and indications by which a man may know when they proceed from one cause and when from another would be somewhat difficult, as also to give examples and indications. It is quite possible, however, to give some general signs, which are these.

When in its words and conceptions the soul finds itself loving God, and at the same time is conscious not only of love but also of humility and reverence, it is a sign that the Holy Spirit is working within it, for, whenever He grants favors, He grants them with this accompaniment.

When the locutions proceed solely from the vivacity and brilliance of the understanding, it is the understanding that accomplishes everything, without the operation of the virtues (although the will, in the knowledge and illumination of those truths, may love naturally); and, when the meditation is over, the will remains dry, albeit inclined neither to vanity nor to evil, unless the devil should tempt it afresh about this matter. This, however, is not the case when the locutions have been prompted by a good spirit; for then, as a rule, the will is afterwards affectionate to God and inclined to well-doing.

At certain times, nevertheless, it will happen that, although the communication has been the work of a good spirit, the will remains in aridity, since God ordains it so for certain causes that are of assistance to the soul. At other times the soul will not be very conscious of the operations or motions of those virtues, yet that which it has experienced will be good. Wherefore I say that the difference between these locutions is sometimes difficult to recognize, by reason of the varied effects which they produce; but these which have now been described are the most common, although sometimes they occur in greater abundance and sometimes in less.

But those that come from the devil are sometimes difficult to understand and recognize, for, although it is true that as a rule they leave the will in aridity with respect to love of God, and the mind inclined to vanity, self-esteem or complacency, nevertheless they sometimes inspire the soul with a false humility and a fervent affection of the will rooted in self-love, so that at times a person must be extremely spiritually-minded to recognize it. And this the devil does in order the better to protect himself; for he knows very well how sometimes to produce tears by the feelings which he inspires in a soul, in order that he may continue to implant in it the affections that he desires. But he always strives to move its will so that it may esteem those interior communications, attach great importance to them, and, as a result, give itself up to them and be occupied in that which is not virtue, but is rather the occasion of losing virtue as the soul may have.[186]

Not infrequently, he manages to hide his traps amongst the joys and delights of moral goods, such as works of mercy, observance of God's will, kindness, and gentility.[187] St. John is not saying that such works are occasions of sin, rather that there is a danger that we might congratulate ourselves and become complacent and vain.

Very great are the benefits which come to the soul when it desires not to set the vain rejoicing of its will on this kind of good. For, in the first place, it is freed from falling into many temptations and deceits of the devil, which are involved in rejoicing in these good works,….. this rejoicing; for, apart altogether from his suggestions, vain rejoicing is itself deception. This is especially true when there is any boasting of heart concerning these good works.[188]

The devil might also propose the heroic deeds of the saints – not only for our edification, but to set us up for failure. What the saints have in common is not the imitation of each other, but the imitation of Christ according to their proper state in life. Then the devil goes on to present to these people their own virtues, slight imperfections for good measure, and then their virtues again, making them think they are already converted and perfect.

St. John also mentions that the evil can use images of saints in churches, making it appear as if extraordinary things were happening to them or through them. The devil does this to deceive and then harm the faith of the people of God. Above all, indiscreet people are more prone to being fooled by such things.[189]

-7-

The Devil's Strategies

Satan's Easiest Prey

As we have seen, people who have a certain fascination for the extraordinary are frequently targets of the Evil One.

Arousal of the Corporal Senses

With regard to the sense appetites, the Evil One can easily excite them to rebel.[190]

Where the Devil May Not Tread

On the other hand, the devil is incapable of moving the will directly, but influences it indirectly by way of his action on perceptions, corporeal apprehensions, etc. but only in their first movements, since it is ultimately up to the individual to make his choice: to resist or consent.[191]

All of the above is useful in the hands of the devil to incite a person's will to thoughts of vanity and self-satisfaction.[192] But he might also succeed in getting the person to fault against charity,[193] or commit sins of avarice, anger, or envy,[194] or spiritual gluttony.[195]

Offensive Attack

Satan does not arrive at the battleground unarmed. To understand the nature of his offensive we need to understand what weapons he uses, his tactics, and the phases *of battle* according to which he develops his strategic plan.

Weapons and armaments

Sacred Scripture often refers to the devil in bellicose terms. St. John of the Cross writes in similar terms.[196] There are a variety of weapons, including: sensuality, corporal visions, and intellectual visions.

In regards to sensuality, John refers to the Beast of the Apocalypse (12:17) referring to the seven heads as the seven antitheses of the degrees of love.[197] The first "head" refers to those sensual things of the world;[198] in other words, those things that enter the soul *naturally* by way of the external senses. Here St. John of the Cross means all those sense apprehensions and sensible pleasures of temporal things.[199]

The second weapon consists of corporeal visions and their communications. In other words, he points to those things that can be presented to the soul *supernaturally* by way of the five external senses.[200]

With the third head, St. John means the interior sense powers.[201] These include those things beyond imagined corporeal apprehensions; i.e., natural or supernatural thoughts and what goes on in the imaginative memory.[202]

The fourth, fifth, sixth, and seventh heads represent those spiritual apprehension already mentioned: visions of corporeal substances, "revelations," "locutions," and spiritual sentiments in the will respectively. His arsenal contains: interior words,[203] thoughts, [204] intellectual ideas,[205] concepts,[206] reasonings,[207] imagined discourses,[208] graphic thoughts or fogginess of mind and senses,[209] appetites joined to thoughts,[210] carnal movements,[211] disquiet and irksomeness in sense and spirit,[212] torments, pain, and darkness,[213] dryness and oppressions,[214] scruples, confusion, fear,[215] interior and external terrors, spiritual fear,[216] and external noises and disturbances.[217]

Relative efficacy: St. John of the Cross is quick to assure us that those weapons the devil uses against us of a more spiritual nature have less efficacy than those that work on the senses.[218] As a result, the most effective weapons the devil has at his disposal are those that involve phantasms and the pleasure of the senses.[219]

Using phantasms, the devil gains influence over the soul. His worst deceits often involve phantasms and those things stored up in the memory.[220] It is precisely there, in the interior senses, where he wreaks the greatest amount of havoc, since the other powers of the soul depend on this aspect of the mind.[221] If the internal senses were hermetically sealed, and if the memory were able to annihilate all of its phantasms, the devil would never be able to work on the mind since he would have nothing to use against the person.[222]

Similarly, by way of the sense appetites Satan ensnares the soul and keeps it from the freedom that the love of God brings.[223] Nonetheless, if the soul is schooled in mortification and abnegation and the desire for sense pleasures has been snuffed out, neither the devil nor the world, nor the flesh have weapons enough to vanquish the power of the Holy Spirit in such a soul.[224]

Tactics

As the person progresses on the path of configuration with Christ, growing in desire for him, allowing himself to be transformed and cooperating with this transformation, the devil adapts his tactics. St. John of the Cross identifies three particular tactics the enemy of human nature uses: deception, wiles, suggestion.

Although these might seem to be mere synonyms their Sanjuanistic use seems to reveal slight differences. He uses these three words quite frequently. The difference seems to be their material function. All of the devil's activity ultimately seeks the spiritual frustration and destruction of God's children. But his ways are many and not all of them imply the equal intensity.

Deception:[225] Just as it is difficult to find the word "sin" in all of St. John of the Cross' writings (he prefers to use the word "appetite" – and this word is found quite frequently), the most frequently used word from John's pen to describe the devil's activity is "deception." Deception is the entry level work of the devil - basic and useful for his interests. This deception takes different forms which are reflected in St. John's synonymous usage of the concept: transfiguration,[226] simulation,[227] masquerade,[228] feint,[229] lead into error,[230] lie,[231] and provoke credulity.[232]

John has many other synonyms for demonic deceit, albeit sharing a common goal: to spiritually damage the person made according to the image and likeness of God, leading him to truncate his spiritual life and commit evil. If he manages to plant his roots deeply he can more easily work on the intellective powers of the soul.[233]

Of course, his insinuations are subtle and clever. The way he works on a person is determined, in great part, by where that person is situated on the path of faith. It makes no sense to present a temptation to commit grave evils to someone who would be repulsed by it. In other words, he works under the guise of goodness, since an attempt to present a manifest evil would only confirm the person in his decision for Christ. Therefore, he conforms himself to each person, attempting to imitate how the Lord deals with these people,[234] even if he is only capable of coming up with a cheap imitation.[235] As a result, he works on the exterior senses with representations similar to the things of God.[236]

With regard to the interior senses he often presents experiences similar to those communicated by God.[237]

Deceits that touch the intellect are distinguished from those of God in that they are abstruse, complicated, convoluted, and ultimately lead to spiritual pitfalls. He will use many words, often similar to those of our Lord, convincing the person with a multitude of lies.[238]

Wiles[239]: If "deception" is garden variety diabolical activity, his "wiles," at least according to John's use of the term, imply a pregnant evil which is more refined. They are the dangerous passes through which we all must walk on the path of faith and, therefore, the logical places for him to set his ambush.

Wiles deal with weaknesses. As a result, they take into account our likes and dislikes and focus in great part on the passage from sense to spirit.[240] There he lays low to attack the person in both of these areas. Often the devil will use the very means that bring relief and remedy to body and soul, since those things that are objectively evil would never pose an attraction to this person.[241]

For example, if someone were to have authentic supernatural experiences (of a divine origin, that is), the devil will tempt such a person "in many ways"[242] leading that person to a disordered attachment to affections and appetites, both spiritual and sensual. The term St. John uses is "spiritual gluttony."

For not only can he represent to the memory and the fancy many false forms and ideas, which seem true and good, impressing them on spirit and sense with great effectiveness and certifying them to be true by means of suggestion (so that it appears to the soul that it cannot be otherwise, but that everything is even as he represents it; for, as he transfigures himself into an angel of light, he appears as light to the soul); but he may also tempt the soul in many ways with respect to true knowledge, which is of God, moving its desires and affections, whether spiritual or sensual, in unruly fashion with respect to these; for, if the soul takes pleasure in such apprehensions, it is very easy for the devil to cause its desires and affections to grow within it, and to make it fall into spiritual gluttony and other evils.[243]

Notice how the devil convinces the person that the origin of such experiences could not be anything outside of God given the attractiveness of the experience, the delight that accompanies it, and the truth of the "prophecies" revealed to the person.

One might ask how a demon can aid someone in knowing future contingencies or why a demon would grant someone such delightful spiritual experiences. Thomas tells us:

A demon's act is twofold. One comes of deliberate will; and this is properly called his own act. Such an act on the demon's part is always wicked; because, although at times he does something good, yet he does not do it well; as when he tells the truth in order to deceive; and when he believes and confesses, yet not willingly, but compelled by the evidence of things. Another kind of act is natural to the demon; this can be good and bears witness to the goodness of nature. Yet he abuses even such good acts to evil purpose.[244]

Once the demon has produced such an experience and brought the person to a degree of interior quiet he has won the person's confidence, he has a foot in the door.

By way of a series of inner locutions he is able to soften the person's psychology, even bringing the person to tears of consolation with the sentiments he inspires. He uses these spiritual sweets to camouflage his activity, and better prepare the way for the affections he wants to later engender. St. John teaches:

> But those that come from the devil are sometimes difficult to understand and recognize, for, although it is true that as a rule they leave the will in aridity with respect to love of God, and the mind inclined to vanity, self-esteem or complacency, nevertheless they sometimes inspire the soul with a false humility and a fervent affection of the will rooted in self-love, so that at times a person must be extremely spiritually-minded to recognize it. And this the devil does in order to better to protect himself; for he knows very well how sometimes to produce tears by the feelings which he inspires in a soul, in order that he may continue to implant in it the affections that he desires. But he always strives to move its will so that it may esteem those interior communications, attach great importance to them, and, as a result, give itself up to them and be occupied in that which is not virtue, but is rather the occasion of losing virtue as the soul may have.[245]

Further on, St. John says:

> When... the words and communications are of the devil, it comes to pass that the soul responds with more ease and readiness to things that are of greater weight, and for lowlier things it conceives repugnance.[246]

How does one distinguish this from divine activity or even from one's own psychology? St. John of the Cross tells us.

Signs of God's Work in the Soul: St. John of the Cross certainly uses the term "suggestion" to describe the Evil One's strategy, nonetheless he does not do a very good job of describing what form it takes in all of its inner working on the psychology. Despite this, if we look at his usage of the term we can acquire a less murky understanding of what he has to teach us.

Just as deceit and wiles, so too is "suggestion" more than a mere garden variety temptation. What distinguishes suggestion is the way the Evil One dresses these up and the tactics he uses in these instances. Suggestion can take place in diverse circumstances: Satan's efficacy in suggesting things to people is, in great part, determined by that person's goodness or wickedness. Certainly, good people can fall prey to them but the effects of them cannot compare to those things the devil communicates to evil people.[247] On this matter, Aquinas says:

> The temptation which comes from the enemy takes the form of a suggestion, as Gregory says (Hom. xvi in Evang.). Now a suggestion cannot be made to everybody in the same way; it must arise from those things towards which each one has an inclination. Consequently, the devil does not straight away tempt the spiritual man to grave sins, but he begins with lighter sins, so as gradually to lead him to those of greater magnitude.[248]

Nonetheless, even though the devil does not suggest every sin, everyone who commits himself to sin subjects himself to the devil. Thomas continues:

> Therefore, in the same way, the first sin of the devil, who "sinneth from the beginning" (1 John 3:8), is held out to all to be followed, and some imitate at his suggestion, and some of their

own will without any suggestion.[249]

If the wicked have the devil as their head, the good ought not get complacent, says St. John of the Cross. For they too, can fall prey to his suggestions.[250] Thomas agrees: "Now temptation which comes from an enemy can be without sin: because it comes about by merely outward suggestion."[251]

Indeed, even our Lord, says St. John of the Cross, was made the object of diabolical suggestion when, at the end of his forty days' fast, he was presented with a vision of all the kingdoms of the world (*cfr.* Mt 4:8).[252] Some say that all the temptations took place in the desert. Of these, some say that Christ was led into the Holy City, not really, but in an imaginary vision.[253]

In light of this, it becomes clear that suggestion is as effective as the person is configured to Christ. In the case of those persons who have made a pact with Satan, diabolical suggestion becomes extremely efficacious. [254]

With regard to the faculties of the soul in which suggestion occurs, St. John offers us only a few examples: in the senses, in the spirit, appetites, and the intellect:

From all that has been said above it may be clearly understood and inferred how great is the evil that may come to the soul from the devil by way of these supernatural apprehensions.

St. John does not seem to explicitly mention suggestion as an occurrence in the will – the closest he comes to it is referring to diabolical influence on the "sentiments." Yet, he probably refers to sentiments in the context of appetites:

The devil finds it pleasing to suggest to souls and impress on them apprehensions and feelings. As a result of all this, these proficients are easily charmed and beguiled if they are not careful to renounce such apprehensions and feelings and energetically defend themselves through faith.[255]

And, in order the better to do this, he is wont to suggest and give pleasure, sweetness and delight to the senses with respect to these same things of God, so that the soul is corrupted and bewildered[509] by that sweetness, and is thus blinded with that pleasure and sets its eyes on pleasure rather than on love (or, at least, very much more than upon love), and gives more heed to the apprehensions than to the detachment and emptiness which are found in faith and hope and love of God.[256]

On the other hand, St. John of the Cross makes no mention of diabolical suggestion in the reality of exterior senses, even if he does use the phrase "speak with suggestion,"[257] nonetheless, the context of this usage is not the spoken word perceived by auditory sense, but interior locutions taking place in the intellect. In other words, rather than voices, he is speaking of concepts or words communicated by way of suggestion: subtle, false reasonings by which Satan informs the intellects of heretics and heresiarchs.

-8-

Diabolical Attacks on Those in the Purgative Stage

It is difficult to sufficiently stress how frightened the devil is of one's spiritual progress. Happy the soul that can fight against that beast of the Apocalypse, which has seven heads, set over against these seven steps of love, and which makes war therewith against each one, and strives therewith against the soul in each of these mansions, wherein the soul is being exercised and is mounting step by step in the love of God.

And undoubtedly if it strives faithfully against each of these heads, and gain the victory, it will deserve to pass from one step to another, and from one mansion to another, even unto the last, leaving the beast vanquished after destroying its seven heads, wherewith it made so furious a war upon it. So furious is this war that Saint John says in that place that it was given unto the beast to make war against the saints and to be able to overcome them upon each one of these steps of love, arraying against each one many weapons and munitions of war.[258]

St. John is clearly referring to the seven mansions that St. Teresa uses to describe spiritual progress. The language of seven stages is only found a couple of times in Sanjuanistic teaching. He adheres to the more traditional three stages of the interior as described by pseudo-Dionysius and most spiritual theologians of the East and West since the Fifth Century: purgative, illuminative, unitive.

Spiritual progress is determined (and revealed) by one's moral and prayer life. How one prays will be, in part, a reflection of the virtuous (or selfish) choices one makes through the day. How well one prays will, in part, also determine one's ability to cooperate with grace in making those choices. For the generous person, this becomes a virtuous circle.

On the other hand, St. John of the Cross laments that "many who engage in this spiritual battle against the beast do not even destroy its first head by denying themselves the sensual things of the world. And, though some destroy and cut off this head, they destroy not the second head, which is that of the visions of sense whereof we are speaking.

> But what is most to be lamented is that some, having destroyed not only the first and the second but even the third, which is that of the interior senses, pass out of the state of meditation, and travel still farther onward, and are overcome by this spiritual beast at the moment of their entering into purity of spirit, for he rises up against them once more, and even his first head comes to life again, and the last state of those souls is worse than the first, since, when they fall back, the beast brings with him seven other spirits worse than himself.[259]

Since virtue and prayer form the two poles of Sanjuanistic spiritual doctrine, we will concentrate on what he has to say about demonic influence on those two areas in each of the three stages of the spiritual life.

Against Novices (those in the purgative stage)

This is a stage of spiritual infancy. God treats them in the same way the best of mothers treats her child,[260] and does not expect much more from them than the virtue proper to children,[261] weak and imperfect,[262] operating, not out of true conviction but on account of the spiritual joy they receive[263] and the consolations resulting from their good choices.[264]

With that in mind, it makes sense that the evil one will take advantage of these imperfect disposition in order to tempt them.[265] People in the purgative stage are tempted to pride upon experiencing sensible fervor resulting from their exercise of new-found piety and prayer. Often, they experience a hidden self-esteem and self-satisfaction when considering their own good works.

Diabolical attacks are to be expected. In fact, the devil can give increase to the sensible fervor experienced by the novice, fomenting a strong desire to multiply his good works. As this desire increases, so does the danger of falling into presumption – precisely what the Evil One has in mind. In other words, his goal is to transform such works, desires, and feelings into vice.[266] St. John says that the devil will even create false ecstasies in these people – albeit, more often than not in public, than in private[267] - because he is well aware of their vain self-complacency and long to be "caught" by others in such a state.[268]

With regard to lust, novices undergo many trials of the flesh, even when recollected, in prayer, approaching going to Communion or confession.[269] It seems that their sensible fervor has been so piqued and their habit of self-dominion grace so new, that they have difficult time knowing what to do with all of these feelings.

To bring disquietude and disturbance on a soul when it is praying, or trying to pray, he endeavors to excite impure feelings in the sensory part. And if people pay any attention to these, the devil does them great harm. Through fear, some souls grow slack in their prayer - which is what the devil wants - in order to struggle against these movements, and others give it up entirely, for they think these feelings come while they are engaged in prayer rather than at other times. And this is true because the devil excites these feelings while souls are at prayer, instead of when they are engaged in other works, so that they might abandon prayer. And that is not all; to make them cowardly and afraid, he brings vividly to their minds foul and impure thoughts. And sometimes the thoughts will concern spiritually helpful things and persons. Those who attribute any importance to such thoughts, therefore, do not even dare look at anything or think about anything lest they thereupon stumble into them.

These impure thoughts so affect people who are afflicted with melancholia that one should have great pity for them; indeed, these people suffer a sad life. In some who are troubled with this bad humor the trial reaches such a point that they clearly feel that the devil has access to them without their having the freedom to prevent it. Yet some of these melancholiacs are able through intense effort and struggle to forestall this power of the devil.

If these impure thoughts and feelings arise from melancholia, individuals are not ordinarily freed from them until they are cured of that humor - unless they enter the dark night, which in time deprives them of everything.[270]

Spiritual gluttony is common among novices in the spiritual life. A great deal can be said on spiritual gluttony, the fourth vice. There are hardly any persons among these beginners, no matter how excellent their conduct, who do not fall into some of the many imperfections of this vice. These imperfections arise because of the delight beginners find in their spiritual exercises.[271]

As contradictory as it might seem, these beginners in the spiritual life sometimes experience such spiritual delight in their corporal penance which, unchecked, can sink into carnal pleasure. For St. John, the key to a healthy life of asceticism is its intention and submissiveness to in obedience to one's spiritual director. The danger here for the novice is his own self-assurance that he is pleasing God so much with his pious and penitential indiscretions (how could it be any other way, he is pleasing himself to no end?!) that he will outwardly accept what his spiritual director says, but legalistically modify his own behavior in order to continue doing what he was already doing.[272] When called to accounts again by his spiritual director, this person gets angry, defensive, complains of being misunderstood.[273]

Above all, the attacks a novice experiences in the area of prayer are indirect, usually regarding the senses. Satan excites disordered movements in the sense in order to "disquiet and bother the soul at prayer or preparing to pray."[274]

St. John of the Cross says that this is a fight the enemy often wins. The person who wants to pray well or, indeed, is already at prayer, experiences rebellions of the flesh and, fulfilling exactly what the devil intended, interrupts his prayer to fight against the temptation, instead of calmly continuing his prayer and not paying attention to the temptation. These people often fall into discouragement as a result of such experiences and hesitate to advance along the way of perfection. They do not make the connection that the enemy is at work, sowing these temptations more often during prayer than outside of it. They wonder if they will ever make progress.[275]

It will be recalled, as seen in chapter 4, the prayer life of a novice consists of vocal prayer and discursive meditation. In other words, there is a predominance of accentuated activity in the interior senses, so much so that purgative stage has as one of its goals to bring the person from imaginative prayer and sensory meditation to a more spiritual prayer – contemplation.[276]

When the Lord decides to elevate the person and free him from the lowly prayer of senses and imagined discourses, then begins the crisis of the passive night of the senses.[277] Such persons are at a loss, so much so that they do not know how to pray in this new place of darkness. Their imaginative sense is confounded.[278]

The period of transition is visited by dryness and temptations of all sorts[279] with differing lengths of trial in different people, according to the heights to which our Lord wills to elevate them.[280] St. John identifies three possible trials during this phase of prayer: attacks by the spirits of fornication, blasphemy, and loathing.

An angel of Satan [2 Cor. 12:7], which is the spirit of fornication, is given to some to buffet their senses with strong and abominable temptations and afflict their spirit with foul thoughts and very vivid images, which sometimes is a pain worse than death for them.[281]

At other times a blasphemous spirit is added; it commingles intolerable blasphemies with all one's thoughts and ideas. Sometimes these blasphemies are so strongly suggested to the imagination that the soul is almost made to pronounce them, which is a grave torment to it.[282]

Sometimes another loathsome spirit, which Isaiah calls *spiritus vertiginis* [Is. 19:14], is sent to these souls, not for their downfall but to try them. This spirit so darkens the senses that such souls are filled with a thousand scruples and perplexities, so intricate that such persons can never be content with anything, nor can their judgment receive the support of any counsel or idea. This is one of the most burdensome goads and horrors of this night - very similar to what occurs in the spiritual night. [283]

Indeed, St. Teresa of Avila agrees. "Innumerable are the obstacles placed in the way of the beginner by the devil. His goal is to impede their progress along this road." [284] "In fact, the devil places so many snares and dangers in their way that one requires not a little bit of courage – beyond the immense help God provides - in order to not make an about-face and give up." [285] Sometimes these attacks involve tremendous violence and provoke a profound sorrow:

> In truth, the violence was so intolerable that the demon and bad habits did not allow me to dedicate myself to prayer. Such was the sadness this brought about that it would catch me whenever I entered the oratory, so much so that I was forced to plea with all my might." [286]

She goes on to say how the Tempter incites a sort of spiritual lust in the person dedicated to prayer, as a sort of cheap imitation of the delights enjoyed by those advanced along the ways of prayer: "There was also a very common temptation which consisted of desiring the joys and peace of prayer as soon as I had begun…. This was a work of the devil." [287]

Temptations are multiform. This underscores how much the devil hates the one who prays, and he exerts much energy to bring someone along mistaken ways of prayer in order to keep the person from objectively approaching God. "The deceits and the wiles of the devil are horrible as the devil attempts to prohibit the person from knowing oneself and realizing what is going on along this path." [288] To advance means to work, to tire oneself, fighting along the way. To progress means to undergo all sorts of turbation and trials. "It is not our lot to be angels here below, that is not our nature. As a result, I am not bothered when I see a soul vexed by grave temptations." [289]

St. Thomas Aquinas affirms that not all temptations come from the devil.[290] Nonetheless, Teresa reminds us, the Tempter takes advantage of them all, profiting from our weakness and instigating still more.

> The more temptations you undergo, the less you should worry about them, since it often regards weakness of the imagination or bad humors. The devil, realizing this, does his part to take advantage of them."[291]

Worldlings enjoy a certain peace since they are left alone by the devil who has no need to seek their perdition further. They do a fine job of it themselves. He leaves them alone because he knows that the words of Christ are true: he who is not with God is against him (Lk 11:23).

> Whoever has given himself over to the world, with habits of grave sin, lives with much tranquility, free of all bother regarding his vices. His conscience no longer bites him and this peace is a sign that the devil and he are friends. So long as he lives in this way, the devil will leave him alone. He sees no reason to wage war on him.[292]

St. Teresa recognizes in the flesh yet another ally of the devil.

> There is a lot to say about the peace and damage brought about by sins of the flesh. I will simply make the following points from which you can deduce the rest: our flesh, as you know, loves comfort and we ought to realize how dangerous it is for our souls to seek peace between our flesh and comfort.[293]

Rather than leave our post on the battlefield and seek out a false peace, St. Teresa invites us to renew our desire to fight for the cause of Christ:

They are like soldiers who are only happy when they fight, assured they will come out victorious.[294] The soldiers of Christ, that is, those who have been elevated to contemplation and practice prayer, do not see the hour of battle, nor do they fear their declared enemies."[295]

But for those who have not advanced, the spiritual life is arduous combat: "The amount of attacks and assaults heaped upon the (novice) in a thousand ways are terrible."[296]

-9-

Diabolical Attacks on Those in the Illuminative Stage

Having left the purgative way behind, the person embarks upon wholly new terrain, incomparable to what he has experienced thus far.[297] As we saw in Chapter 4, this new phase is marked by a predominance of the spirit, is also called the way of the proficient, and includes affective prayer which prepares the soul for the prayer of simplicity, a precursor to infused contemplation, with the possibility of brief, if infrequent, moments of infused contemplation.[298]

Normally this phase lasts a long time – many years, in fact,[299] during which the soul is prepared for the arduous and transforming dark night of the spirit, passing through the narrow lanes of divine love.[300]

In the *Spiritual Canticle*, John of the Cross explains three different kinds of diabolic temptations which affect advanced spiritual souls: First, those that vehemently incite the imagination; second, when the first way proves futile, bodily torments and noises that distract the soul; and third, still worse, the sometimes frightful torment of the devil struggling against the soul with spiritual terrors and horrors. The Spanish saint gives little detail of the second category of temptations, although as we read in biographies of his life, he was affected by them (P. Crisogono de Jesus Sacramentado 111).

In the case of spiritual horrors, "the devil can do this easily, for since the soul at this time enters into great nakedness of spirit for the sake of this spiritual exercise, the devil can easily show himself to her, because he is also spirit" (Spiritual Canticle 476). His mysterious presence poses intriguing psychological and spiritual problems.[301]

The devil, who in his great malice is envious of all the good he sees in the soul, knowing of her prosperity, now employs all his ability and engages all his crafts to disturb this good, even if only a slight part of it. It is worth more to him to hinder a small fraction of this soul's rich and glorious delight than to make many others fall into numerous serious sins, for these others have little or nothing to lose; but this soul has very much to lose because of all her precious gain. The loss of a little pure gold is much worse than the loss of many other base metals.[302]

What occurs during this phase is similar to what St. John of the Cross describes previous to spiritual marriage, which occurs during the unitive phase. As a result, it behooves us to accurately distinguish the influence of the evil spirit in his accidental aspect during this phase, such as the secondary mystical phenomena in contrast to those direct assaults against its epicenter and nucleus, which is contemplation.

Secondary Phenomena

These are made up of those supernatural communications which often, though not necessarily, accompany mystical evolution: i.e., visions, locutions, the revelation of hidden mysteries, spiritual sentiments, etc.[303] Many proficients enjoy a tide of visions, in the senses as well as in the spirit: nonetheless, these more often than not take place in the imagination than in the exterior senses.[304]

Wherefore we shall now begin to treat of those other four apprehensions of the understanding, which, as we said in the tenth chapter, are purely spiritual -- namely, visions, revelations, locutions and spiritual feelings. These we call purely spiritual, for they do not (as do those that are corporeal and imaginary) communicate themselves to the understanding by way of the corporeal senses; but, without the intervention of any inward or outward corporeal sense, they present themselves to the understanding, clearly and distinctly, by supernatural means, passively -- that is to say, without the performance of any act or operation on the part of the soul itself, at the least actively.

It must be known, then, that, speaking broadly and in general terms, all these four apprehensions may be called visions of the soul; for we term the understanding of the soul also its sight. And since all these apprehensions are intelligible to the understanding, they are described, in a spiritual sense, as 'visible.' And thus the kinds of intelligence that are formed in the understanding may be called intellectual visions.[305] Throughout all of this Satan does not remain idle.

They receive an abundance of spiritual communications and apprehensions in the sensory and spiritual parts of their souls and frequently behold imaginative and spiritual visions. All of this as well as other delightful feelings are the lot of those who are in this state, and a soul is often tricked through them by its own phantasy as well as by the devil. The devil finds it pleasing to suggest to souls and impress on them apprehensions and feelings. As a result of all this, these proficients are easily charmed and beguiled if they are not careful to renounce such apprehensions and feelings and energetically defend themselves through faith.

> This is the stage in which the devil induces many into believing vain visions and false prophecies. He strives to make them presume that God and the saints speak with them, and frequently they believe their phantasy. It is here that the devil customarily fills them with presumption and pride. Drawn by vanity and arrogance, they allow themselves to be seen in exterior acts of apparent holiness, such as raptures and other exhibitions. They become audacious with God and lose holy fear, which is the key to and guardian of all the virtues. Illusions and deceptions so multiply in some, and they become so inveterate in them, that it is very doubtful whether they will return to the pure road of virtue and authentic spirituality. They fall into these miseries by being too secure in their surrender to these apprehensions and spiritual feelings and do this just when they were beginning to make progress along the way.[306]

Given what St. John says above, we understand why so few people actually pass from the illuminative stage to the unitive. The devil does not limit his influence to visions and corporeal apprehensions, but also has recourse to spiritual communications to exercise his influence.[307]

If he perceives that God or a good angel is blessing the soul with communications, he will attempt to spoil this interior feast. His tactic is to meet spiritual experience with spiritual experience,[308] enjoying a relative success as a result and sometimes finding his advances completely rebuffed.

In fact, says St. John of the Cross, the advanced soul often vanquishes the foe in such a way that he causes the devil such distress causing him to flee in confusion – especially, if the proficient makes contemplation his hiding place, thus advancing spiritually and winning for himself more grace which God is happy to grant him.

Not only does the devil imitate this kind of corporeal vision, but he also simulates and interferes with spiritual communications coming from a good angel, since he can discern them, as we said; and as Job said, *omne sublime videt* "He sees every sublime thing" [Jb. 41:25], imitates and interferes with them. Yet he cannot imitate and form these spiritual communications as he can those granted under some appearance or figure, for these are without form and figure, and it is of the nature of the spirit to be formless and figureless. He represents his frightful spirit to the soul in order to attack it in the same way in which it receives the spiritual communication, and to assail and destroy the spiritual with the spiritual. In this case, when the good angel communicates spiritual contemplation, the soul cannot enter the hiding place of this contemplation quickly enough to go unnoticed by the devil. He then presents himself to it with some spiritual horror and disturbance, at times very painful. Sometimes the soul can withdraw speedily without giving this horror of the evil spirit an opportunity to make an impression on it, and it recollects itself by the efficacious favor the good angel then gives it.[309] Inconstancy of vigilance opens a breach for the enemy:

At other times the devil prevails, and disturbance and horror seize upon it. This terror is a greater suffering than any other torment in life. Since this horrendous communication proceeds from spirit to spirit manifestly and somewhat incorporeally, it surpasses all sensory pain. This spiritual suffering does not last long, for if it did the soul would depart from the body on account of this violent communication. Afterward the soul can recall this diabolic communication; doing so is enough to cause great suffering.[310]

As we have seen, an essential element of the mystical life is the divine invasion - an inflowing and influence of grace that transforms the soul.[311] In its first purgative phase the presence of God is purgative and painful, working toward the passive night of the spirit. Continued growth on the way to union, the soul undergoes illumination of the intellect[312] and a loving inflammation of the spirit,[313] making the soul catch fire bringing it to become fire itself, just as a cold, damp log submitted to flame over time becomes one with the fire. This is the transformation our Lord seeks for us: to be divinized.[314]

The soul in this phase exercises no more imagination and discursive meditation in its prayer. Rather, it progresses along the ways of divine love with broader steps, greater satisfaction, and increased generosity,[315] nourished and renewed by the Lord without exerting nearly as much personal effort as before.[316]

According to Teresa, the devil takes more pains to bring about the downfall of a soul receiving graces from God in prayer than in less-favored souls. This is also the opinion of John of the Cross who says that the devil accomplishes more through a little harm caused to an advanced soul than great damage to many others.

Like a good captain, a holy soul leads many others to heaven and does the devil much harm. Such a holy soul's special love of God is sufficient to make the devil do his utmost to bring about perdition. The conflict, then, is sterner for such a soul than for one who is less holy.[317]

Witnessing this progress the Evil One experiences tremendous envy and pain.[318] Recognizing the signs of spiritual peace, prosperity, interior recollection with which the Holy Spirit delicately blesses this person, the Evil One flies into a rage of disgust.[319] Witnessing the fruits of the blessings – the devil is blind to the economy of grace, therefore, he can only see its effects - he is reminded of those things he has freely refused. The good things of God he has rejected he wants to hinder in those who cooperate with grace. The spiritual growth of the proficient is a torture for the devil.[320] About this Thomas tells us:

Now the envious man repines over the good possessed by another, inasmuch as he deems his neighbor's good to be a hindrance to his own. But another's good could not be deemed a hindrance to the good coveted by the wicked angel, except inasmuch as he coveted a singular excellence, which would cease to be singular because of the excellence of some other. So, after the sin of pride, there followed the evil of envy in the sinning angel, whereby he grieved over man's good, and also over the Divine excellence, according as against the devil's will God makes use of man for the Divine glory.[321]

Demons are so twisted, says St. John of the Cross that "There is no devil who is not willing to suffer something for his own sense of honor."[322] From what we have seen thus far, it is clear that devil has an exaggerated sense of himself. People who take themselves too seriously are rarely happy. The devil is never happy. And all of the demonic assaults we have thus far considered have been peripheral circumventions, so to say, inasmuch as they were indirectly and therefore, more or less successfully, aimed at the stronghold of contemplation. Contemplation constitutes the last bulwark of the spiritual edifice, which will determine the demon's twisted honor or confusion in spiritual combat.

John of the Cross writes of these experiences, observing that the devil causes the greatest harm and makes the soul lose abundant riches by alluring it with a little bait out of the simple waters of the spirit. Teresa had similar experiences, finding that this sort of temptation usually occurs with contemplative souls who find themselves in the "fifth mansion;" the mansion characterized by the contemplative prayer of union with God.[323]

Considering what St. John of the Cross has to say about how the devil attempts to hinder contemplation we find it laid out succinctly in *The Dark Night of the Soul* (book 2, chapter 23), *Spiritual Canticle* (chapters 16 and 18), and *The Living Flame of Love* (chapter 3). Reading these texts next to each other we discover a beautiful complementarity in which the spiritual doctrine of one text illumines the content of the others. From the contents of these chapters we will limit ourselves to consider the following notions: objectives, tactics, attacks.

The proximate objective consists of defending the wall of contemplation so that the soul may not enter,[324] because within lies the hiding place of recollection where the soul is alone with its divine Spouse.[325] The devil knows that once the soul enters this place he will find it nearly impossible to harm it.[326] Satan commands his demons to do everything possible to block the passage to contemplation [327] and impede advances.[328]

The devil attacks the sensed part of the soul in order to impede secret spiritual communications. He knows well that the encounter of these two lovers, the soul and its Spouse – the only begotten Word of God – requires solitude and detachment from everything.[329] As a result, all of the senses and their interior and exterior powers must come to rest, be emptied, and in a state of quiet.[330] In order to impede the soul's entrance into the fortress of contemplation the devil will attempt to disquiet and disturb the person[331] in the different faculties. In this way the devil's attacks are peripheral – not attacking contemplation itself, but those things it requires for success.

In other words, since the evil cannot reach the depths of one's soul,[332] he settles for more superficial attacks on the senses where he can have more success: creating diversions and sowing confusion in hopes of disturbing contemplation and its contingent graces:

It is quite true that even though the devil is ignorant of the nature of these very interior and secret spiritual communications, he frequently perceives that one is receiving them because of the great quietude and silence some of them cause in the sensory part. And since he is aware that he cannot impede them in the depths of the soul, he does everything possible to excite and disturb the sensory part, which he can affect with sufferings, horrors, and fears. He intends by this agitation to disquiet the superior and spiritual part of the soul in its reception and enjoyment of that good.[333]

These are many and take varied forms, albeit they are identical inasmuch as they always attack the sensitive part of the intellect. The practical results of these depends less on the expertise of the aggressor or degree of violence with which he attacks the proficient, than on the degree of foresight of the person under attack and the degree of contemplation achieved.

A first type of spiritual communication is that which is inexplicable without part of the senses. In other words, this is contemplation that is not wholly pure, but still dependent upon the senses and still wrapped up in those activities in the lower parts of the soul:

At other times, when the spiritual communication is not bestowed exclusively on the spirit but on the senses too, the devil more easily disturbs and agitates the spirit with these horrors by means of the senses. The torment and pain he then causes is immense, and sometimes it is ineffable. For since it proceeds nakedly from spirit to spirit, the horror the evil spirit causes within the good spirit (in that of the soul), if he reaches the spiritual part, is unbearable. The bride of the Song of Songs also speaks of this disturbance in telling of her desire to descend to interior recollection and enjoy these goods: I went down into the garden of nuts to see the apples of the valleys and if the vineyard was in flower; I knew not; my soul was troubled by the chariots (by the carts and roaring) of Aminadab (the devil) [Sg. 6:11-12].[334]

Juxtaposed to the success the devil has on beginners, his assaults on the senses of the proficient are usually negligible. The proficient have, in most cases, sufficiently mortified their sense to such an extent that whatever demons attempt, it usually comes to nothing or very little.

The devil at this point takes advantage of the sensory appetites, although most of the time he can do very little or nothing, since these appetites are already deadened in persons who have reached this state. When he is unable to stir these appetites, he produces a great variety of images in the imagination. He is sometimes the cause of many movements of the sensory part of the soul and of many other disturbances, spiritual as well as sensory. It is not in a person's power to be free of these until the Lord sends his angel, as is said in the psalm, round about them that fear him and delivers them [Ps. 34:7], and until he brings peace and tranquility in both the sensory and spiritual parts of the soul.[335]

In the face of such a route, the devil does not give up but changes his approach, attacking the phantasy and the imagination and lots of distractions.[336] The least attachment to the created provides an entry for the Evil One.

When the soul is in the loftiest solitudes, receiving the infusion of the delicate unctions of the Holy Spirit insofar as it is alone, despoiled, and withdrawn from every creature and trace of creature, the devil, with great sadness and envy, seeing that the soul is not only enriched but flying along at such a pace that he cannot catch it in anything, strives to intrude in this withdrawal with some clouds of knowledge and sensible satisfaction. This knowledge and satisfaction he gives is sometimes good, so he may feed the soul more and make it revert to particular things and the work of the senses, and make it turn thus to this good knowledge and satisfaction, embrace it, and journey to God leaning upon it.

He consequently distracts it very easily and draws it out of that solitude and recollection in which, as we said, the Holy Spirit is bringing about those secret marvels. Since humans of themselves are inclined toward feeling and tasting, especially if they are seeking something and do not understand the road they are traveling, they easily grow attached to the knowledge and satisfaction provided by the devil and lose the solitude God was providing. Since the soul was doing nothing in that solitude and quiet of the faculties, it thinks that this way is better because it is now doing something.

It is a great pity that, in not understanding itself and for the sake of eating a morsel of particular knowledge and satisfaction, the soul impedes God from feeding on it entirely, which God does in that solitude where he places it, since he absorbs it in himself by means of those solitary spiritual anointings.[337]

Awakening these thoughts, the devil manages to dissipate the contemplative soul and succeeds in undoing the effects of divine communications.[338] As the weakness of the one in the purgative way resides in the lower senses, the proficient's Achilles' heel is in activity – especially in the area of thoughts. If the devil can manage to distract the proficient from his solitary recollection he scores a great victory.

On the other hand, if the devil finds the proficient on guard and not exercising the intellect too much or focused on one thing in particular, his attack becomes even more crass:

At other times, when the spiritual communication is not bestowed exclusively on the spirit but on the senses too, the devil more easily disturbs and agitates the spirit with these horrors by means of the senses. The torment and pain he then causes is immense, and sometimes it is ineffable. For since it proceeds nakedly from spirit to spirit, the horror the evil spirit causes within the good spirit (in that of the soul), if he reaches the spiritual part, is unbearable.[339] If that produces no desired effect, sometimes God grants the devil still more license:

If permission is given them they can do this very easily, for since the soul at this time enters into great nakedness of spirit for the sake of this spiritual exercise, the devil can easily show himself to her, because he is also spirit.[340] Other attacks are: on the rational intellect with "spiritual horrors,"[341] with fear and disturbances,[342] spiritual threats,[343] and disturbing him in times of devotion[344]

St. John of the Cross describes these horrors as "intolerable"; the fear is "tremendous;" the torments and pain are "intense;" and says that these things cannot compare with other crosses life has to offer.[345]

As we have seen, the devil concentrates on the psychosomatic powers of the soul (memory, sensitive appetites, imagination, etc.) as a way to manipulate emotions. Although the Evil One cannot make decisions for somebody else and cannot read their minds, his access to their emotions aids him in the attempt. The memory, says St. John of the Cross, is the devil's playground – especially for those who undergo the dark night of the senses in preparation for the dark night of the spirit.

The devil knows full well that frustrating the prayer life of one advanced along the ways of perfection is more precious a prize than bringing a committed sinner to sin. But he also knows that such a one as that will not be tempted with outright evil, but rather with a false good, something seemingly innocuous which acts as bait. St. Teresa teaches us thus:

> The devil comes with his artful wiles, and, under the color of doing good, sets about undermining it in trivial ways, and working it in practices which, so he gives it to understand, are not wrong. Little by little he darkens the understanding and weakens the will and causes its self-love to increase in one way or another, thus bringing it to withdraw from the love of God and persuade to indulge its own wishes."[346]

The proficient will not be free of these sensitive and spiritual afflictions until the Lord – according to Sacred Scripture[347] - send his angels to those that fear him, thus instilling peace and tranquility in the sense and the spirit.[348]

A second form of spiritual communication is that which is granted to the higher regions of the soul. This contemplation is infused without images, forms, or figures and is expressed without interference of or the imperfections pertaining to the lower parts of the soul. John describes this communication as "confused, dark, and general,"[349] yet at the same time "loving, peaceful, and calm."[350]

When this loving communication is granted with purity and strength, the devil will celebrate no victory in his attempts to disturb the soul absorbed in God.[351] Nonetheless, he does not cease his attacks: the only recourse left for him is to attack the proficient exteriorly: physical assaults, strange noises, and other frightening things.[352]

All of these things Satan does when he sees that the soul is preparing to enter the garden enclosed where the divine Spouse awaits. At all costs he wants to hinder the divine communications that await the contemplative soul.[353] St. John of the Cross, for sure speaking autobiographically, says that as soon as the soul perceives the approach of the demon, almost instinctively and without giving it any thought, it takes refuge in the hiding place of contemplation where it is safe and experiences profound joy.[354]

St. John paints a pathetic image of the devil screaming and pounding on the gate without, furious at the divine communications that are most certainly taking place. Sometimes he remains there for great lengths of time. Finally, upon seeing that he lost that fight, he leaves the soul in complete peace.[355]

The soul, sure in its contemplation, remains in peace with its Spouse. Whatever fears there may have been, they are outside and far away their effect now brings about a new-found joy which St. John describes as "indescribable."[356]

Its peace is more constant and spiritual benefit greater.[357] This new-found situation is something akin to a person in a warm castle, safe and secure, watching a storm outside. The tests are now on the surface: attacks on the body, for sure, but the soul is at peace.[358]

When these favors are bestowed in concealment (only in the spirit, as we said), a person is usually aware, without knowing how, that the superior and spiritual part of the soul is withdrawn and alienated from the lower and sensory part. This withdrawal makes one conscious of two parts so distinct that one seemingly has no relation to the other and is far removed from it. And, indeed, this is in a way true, for in the activity that is then entirely spiritual there is no communication with the sensory part.

A person in this way becomes wholly spiritual, and in these hiding places of unitive contemplation, and by their means, the passions and spiritual appetites are to a great degree eliminated. Referring thus to the superior part, the soul says in this last verse: my house being now all stilled.[359]

For her part, St. Teresa of Avila concurs with her Carmelite brother in much of what he says. She mentions how the soul, advanced along the ways of prayer, is tried in more subtle ways.

> For John of the Cross, a soul which expects to overcome the devil's "strength" will be unable to do so without prayer. Yet to understand his "deceits," the soul needs humility — for the devil is the sworn enemy of humility. The Spanish mystic notes that the devil's bait is pride — especially the pride that arises from spiritual presumption.

> Holy souls must be cautious about any kind of revelations, for the devil usually meddles in them and "joins together so many apparent and appropriate facts, and implants them so firmly in the imagination, that it seems that every event will undoubtedly occur." If the soul has no humility, it will not be torn from its opinion and believe the contrary. Teresa says that demons even use the image of Christ or his saints to foster false devotion. But the visions of the devil do no harm if there is humility:

> 'For my own part, I believe that His Majesty will not allow him, or give him the power, to deceive anyone with such appearances unless the person himself be to blame . . . I mean that for humble souls no deception is possible.' (Foundations, 41)[360]

False humility, on the other hand, proves to be the greatest struggle for the proficient. It can even lead to despair:

I suffered at times—and even still, though not so often—the most grievous trials, together with bodily pains and afflictions arising from violent sicknesses; so much so, that I could scarcely control myself. At other times, my bodily sickness was more grievous; and as I had no spiritual pain, I bore it with great joy: but, when both pains came upon me together, my distress was so heavy, that I was reduced to sore straits.

I forgot all the mercies our Lord had shown me, and remembered them only as a dream, to my great distress; for my understanding was so dull, that I had a thousand doubts and suspicions whether I had ever understood matters aright, thinking that perhaps all was fancy, and that it was enough for me to have deceived myself, without also deceiving good men. I looked upon myself as so wicked as to have been the cause, by my sins, of all the evils and all the heresies that had sprung up. This is but a false humility, and Satan invented it for the purpose of disquieting me, and trying whether he could thereby drive my soul to despair.[361]

St. Teresa calls it "diabolical humility" and uncovers for us its perversity:

I have now had so much experience, that I know this was his work; so he, seeing that I understand him, does not torment me in the same way as much as he used to do. That it is his work is clear from the restlessness and discomfort with which it begins, and the trouble it causes in the soul while it lasts; from the obscurity and distress, the aridity and indisposition for prayer and for every good work, which it produces.[362]

Its fruits work against true humility. She adds:

That other humility, which is the work of Satan, furnishes no light for any good work; it pictures God as bringing upon everything fire and sword; it dwells upon His justice; and the soul's faith in the mercy of God— for the power of the devil does not reach so far as to destroy faith—is of such a nature as to give me no consolation: on the contrary, the consideration of mercies so great helps to increase the pain, because I look upon myself as bound to render greater service.

This invention of Satan is one of the most painful, subtle, and crafty that I have known him to possess; I should therefore like to warn you, my father, of it, in order that, if Satan should tempt you herein, you may have some light, and be aware of his devices, if your understanding should be left at liberty: because you must not suppose that learning and knowledge are of any use here; for though I have none of them myself, yet now that I have escaped out of his hands I see clearly that this is folly. What I understood by it is this: that it is our Lord's pleasure to give him leave and license, as He gave him of old to tempt Job; though in my case, because of my wretchedness, the temptation is not so sharp.[363]

On the other hand,

> True humility is not attended with trouble; it does not disturb the soul; it causes neither obscurity nor aridity: on the contrary, it consoles. It is altogether different, bringing with it calm, sweetness, and light. It is no doubt painful; but, on the other hand, it is consoling, because we see how great is the mercy of our Lord in allowing the soul to have that pain, and how well the soul is occupied. On the one hand, the soul grieves over its offences against God; on the other, His

compassion makes it glad. It has light, which makes it ashamed of itself; and it gives thanks to His Majesty, who has borne with it so long.[364]

-10-
Diabolical Attacks on Those in the Unitive Stage

Those few who arrive at the stage of transforming union are called "perfect" by St. John of the Cross.

Degrees of Prayer in this Phase

Up till now, we have had a glimpse at what the various degrees of prayer life in the purgative and illuminative phases. What follows are a few observations regarding the evolution of prayer in the unitive phase.

Prayer of Quiet: The prayer of quiet is a type of mystical prayer in which the intimate awareness of God's presence captivates the will and fills the soul and body with ineffable sweetness and delight. The fundamental difference between the prayer of quiet and that of infused recollection, apart from the greater intensity of contemplative light and more intense consolations, is that the prayer of quiet gives the soul an actual possession and joyful fruition of the sovereign Good.[365]

St. Teresa describes the prayer of quiet in the following way:

From this recollection there sometimes proceeds an interior quiet and peace that are full of happiness because the soul is in such a state that it does not seem to lack anything, and even speaking [*e.g.,* vocal prayer and meditation] wearies it; it wishes to do nothing but love. This state may last for some time and even for long periods of time.'

The sanctifying effects produced in the soul by the prayer of quiet are enumerated by St. Teresa in the Fourth Mansions of her *Interior Castle*: (1) great liberty of spirit; (2) filial fear of God and great care not to offend him; (3) profound confidence of God; (4) love of mortification and suffering; (5) deep humility; (6) disdain for worldly pleasures; and (7) growth in all the virtues.[366]

Prayer of Union: The prayer of union is that grade of mystical prayer in which all the internal faculties are gradually captivated and occupied with God. In the prayer of quiet only the will was captivated; in the sleep of faculties the intellect was also captivated, although the memory and the imagination remained free. In the prayer of union all the interior faculties, including the memory and the imagination, are captivated. Only the external bodily senses are now free.[367]

The intensity of the mystical experience caused by the prayer of union is indescribable. It is superior beyond compare to that of the preceding grade, to the point that the body itself is affected by the working of God in the soul. Without being entirely captivated, the external senses become almost helpless and inoperative. The person experiences divine reality with such intensity that it could easily fall into ecstasy. At the beginning, this sublime absorption of the faculties in God lasts but a short time (a half hour at most), but as the intensity increases, it may be prolonged for several hours.[368]

Accordingly, the essential characteristics of the prayer of union and the signs by which it can be recognized and distinguished from previous grades of prayer are: an absence of distractions which are psychologically impossible; a certitude of being intimately united with God in which the person cannot doubt that it experiences God during this prayer; and absence of weariness and tedium in which the person is absorbed in God and never wearies of its union with the Beloved, however long it may last.

The Prayer of Conforming Union: While St. Teresa calls this degree of prayerful union with God *the spiritual betrothal or espousal;* others call it the prayer of ecstatic union, taking the name from the primary external phenomenon of this grade. However, Father Aumann, in his classic work, *Spiritual Theology,* prefers to use *conforming union* and *transforming union* for the last two degrees of mystical prayer.

Accordingly, "in the prayer of simple union all the interior faculties of the soul are centered on God alone; only the external senses are still free. But in the prayer of conforming union God captivates even the external senses, with the result that the soul is totally divinized, so to speak, and prepared by God to move to the full and final commitment of the transforming union."[369] Fr. Aumann continues:

> In the prayer of conforming union, therefore, the soul loses the use of its external senses, either partially or totally, because all the interior faculties are absorbed in God and the senses are alienated from their proper natural functioning. It is with difficulty that the soul turns its attention to external activity, though it knows that sometimes it must 'leave God for God' in performing its duties or services of charity for others. But the predominant sentiment of these souls is the longing for full and perfect union with God, accompanied by a longing for death. The soul now echoes the yearning of St. Paul to be dissolved and to be with Christ (Phi.

1:23) and the statement of St. Teresa as a child: 'I want to see God, but to see God we must die.'[370]

In the ecstatic experience of the conforming union, the soul not only has contact with God in the very center of its soul, but also it seems to peer into the very essence of God and discover divine secrets... The soul experiences that it is in God and God in the soul, and the concentration is so complete that all the faculties are absorbed in this union... Mystical ecstasy is therefore a concomitant or normal phenomenon of the prayer of conforming union. Unlike prophetic ecstasy, mystical ecstasy is both sanctifying and meritorious. The essential element in this prayer, however, is the absorption of the soul in God; the ecstasy is a secondary but concomitant element. Both of these elements are necessary for the true mystical ecstasy. Without the union with God in infused contemplative prayer, the ecstasy would be a natural ecstasy or trance, a falsification of mystical ecstasy caused by an evil spirit, or the *gratia gratis data* of prophetic ecstasy.[371]

Prayer of Transforming Union: Fr. Aumann teaches:

The last grade of prayer is the transforming union, identified by many mystics as the spiritual marriage. It constitutes the seventh mansions of *The Interior Castle* of St. Teresa and is the highest degree of perfection that one can attain in this life. It is, therefore, a prelude to the beatific life of glory... In this grade of prayer there is a total transformation of the soul into the Beloved. The soul has entered into its very center, so to speak, which is the throne room of the interior castle where the Trinity dwells through grace. There God and the soul give themselves to each other in the consummation of divine love, so far as is possible in the present life. There is no more ecstasy, for the soul has now been strengthened to receive the full power of love, but in the brightness of an intellectual vision the soul experiences the Trinity with vivid awareness"[372]

We can distinguish three elements in this loftiest degree of the prayer of union: transformation in God, mutual surrender, and the permanent union of love… Concomitant with the permanent union of love is the soul's *confirmation in grace*. St. John of the Cross maintains that the transformation union never falters and the soul is confirmed in grace, but St. Teresa warns that as long as we are in this world we must walk with caution, lest we offend God. However, the apparent contradiction is readily resolved when we say that confirmation in grace does not mean intrinsic impeccability, for the Church teaches that it is an impossibility in this life. Nor is it a question of avoiding all venial sins in this life, for that would require a special privilege of grace as was bestowed on the Virgin Mary. Consequently, confirmation in grace must be understood as the special grace and assistance from God to avoid all mortal sins and thus have moral certificate of salvation.[373]

The Struggle in this Phase

Before the soul is inducted into spiritual marriage, the struggle for definitive union and ruin becomes quite dramatic. As angels come to the aid of the contemplative soul, demons increase their efforts since their time is running out. When divine or angelic communications touch the soul, demons notice something has happened. Although blind to the economy of grace, they see some of the effects and get nervous. "God ordinarily permits the enemy to recognize favors granted through good angels so that he may do what he can, in accord with the measure of justice, to hinder them."[374] In this way, the devil has no room for complaint that he was not afforded an opportunity to try the soul.

Whereas angels produce spiritual communication, demons, in their turn, bring about spiritual horror. These horrors work as a sort of purification of the soul, who, if generous in the face of them, will be richly rewarded. "The soul will enjoy a wondrous and delightful spiritual communication, at times ineffably sublime. The preceding horror of the evil spirit refined the soul so that it could receive this good."[375]

After the person has passed through the bitterness of mortification and the struggles contingent of meditation,[376] after the Lord has brought this person through the periods of anguish, doubts, fear, diabolical visitation and communications,[377] and having been purified at the root[378] by the dark ray,[379] God and the soul become two natures in one spirit and one love.[380]

This spiritual marriage is incomparably greater than the spiritual betrothal, for it is a total transformation in the Beloved, in which each surrenders the entire possession of self to the other with a certain consummation of the union of love. The soul thereby becomes divine, God through participation, insofar as is possible in this life. And thus I think that this state never occurs without the soul's being confirmed in grace, for the faith of both is confirmed when God's faith in the soul is here confirmed. It is accordingly the highest state attainable in this life.[381]

As a result of this new situation for the soul immersed in God and transformed, its relationship with other creatures is, in turn, transformed:

The reason for this security has been clearly explained. Usually a soul never strays except through its appetites, its gratifications, or its discursive meditation, or through its knowledge or affections. By these, people usually fail through excess or defect, or they change because of them or go astray, or experience inordinate inclinations. Once all these operations and movements are impeded, individuals are obviously freed from error in them, because they are not only liberated from themselves but also from their other enemies, the world and the devil. The world and the devil have no other means of warring against the soul when its affections and operations are deadened.[382]

Until now the soul has been purged, illumined, and has entered into spiritual betrothal. Consequently, it was subject to a myriad of attacks, irritations, and vexations – all taking place in the lower regions; yet in a state of spiritual marriage, all of this comes to a halt.[383] Strong in its heroic virtue it no longer engages in spiritual combat, neither against the world, nor the flesh, nor even the devil "who fears to attack her."[384] What interests us now is the soul's reaction to all of this.

But before the soul reaches this full flourishing of spiritual matrimony, it must pass through to the last mansion. In other words, even within the unitive phase, there are trials to undergo:

For Our Lord continues to prove the soul and to raise it ever higher, so that He first gives it things that are very unpretentious and exterior and in the order of sense, in conformity with the smallness of its capacity; to the end that, when it behaves as it should, and receives these first morsels with moderation for its strength and sustenance, He may grant it further and better food.

If, then, the soul conquers the devil upon the first step, it will pass to the second; and if upon the second likewise, it will pass to the third; and so onward, through all seven mansions, which are the seven steps of love, until the Spouse shall bring it to the cellar of wine of His perfect charity.[385] How the soul reacts to these trials will, as always, determine its progress or halt.

And undoubtedly if it strives faithfully against each of these heads, and gain the victory, it will deserve to pass from one step to another, and from one mansion to another, even unto the last, leaving the beast vanquished after destroying its seven heads, wherewith it made so furious a war upon it.[386]

These demonic attacks along the way to transforming union have the undesired effect, in many cases, of helping the soul along in its purification and sanctification. The devil loses twice: his efforts not only fail to impede progress, they help it along.

St. Teresa of Avila offers up supplications for those souls who have achieved union with God, because she well knows that the Evil One transforms himself into an angel of light:

Send me light from Heaven, my Lord, that I may enlighten these your servants, to some of whom you are often pleased to grant these joys, lest, when the devil transfigures himself into an angel of light, he should deceive them, for all their desires are occupied in desiring to please you.[387]

She warns against the subtleties of the Evil One for those in this stage of the spiritual life:

So, Christian souls, whom the Lord has brought to this point on your journey, I beseech you, for His sake, not to be negligent, but to withdraw from occasions of sin -- for even in this state the soul is not strong enough to be able to run into them safely, as it is after the betrothal has been made.[388]

The more a soul advances along the path of holiness, the more precious the prize for the devil should he succeed in bringing one to fall.

I tell you, daughters, I have known people of a very high degree of spirituality who have reached this state, and whom, notwithstanding, the devil, with great subtlety and craft, has won back to himself. For this purpose, he will marshal all the powers of hell, for, as I have often said, if he wins a single soul in this way he will win a whole multitude. The devil has much experience in this matter. If we consider what a large number of people God can draw to Himself through the agency of a single soul, the thought of the thousands converted by the martyrs gives us great cause for praising God. Think of a maiden like Saint Ursula. And of the souls whom the devil must have lost through Saint Dominic and Saint Francis and other founders of Orders, and is losing now through Father Ignatius, who founded the Company - all of whom, of course, as we read, received such favors from God! What did they do but endeavor that this Divine betrothal should not be frustrated through their fault?[389]

The secret is in being attached to the Will of God she says:

[I]f this soul invariably followed the will of God, it is clear that it would not be lost. But the devil comes with his artful wiles, and, under color of doing good, sets about undermining it in trivial ways, and involving it in practices which, so he gives it to understand, are not wrong; little by little he darkens its understanding, and weakens its will, and causes its self-love to increase, until in one way and another he begins to withdraw it from the love of God and to persuade it to indulge its own wishes. And this is also an answer to the second question, for there is no enclosure so strictly guarded that he cannot enter it, and no desert so solitary that he cannot visit it.[390]

St. Teresa speaks often of the devil's deceits regarding visions and the dangers attendant to longing for the extraordinary, insisting that the devil can falsify visions and locutions.[391] Yet, for the perfect, these present little danger, given that they are immersed in the Will of God and not attached to their own. This purity of intention aids them in seeing through malicious deceptions.

> And I shall venture to affirm that, if this is indeed union with God the devil cannot enter or do any harm; for His Majesty is in such close contact and union with the essence of the soul that he will not dare to approach, nor can he even understand this secret thing. That much is evident: for it is said that he does not understand our thoughts; still less, therefore, will he understand a thing so secret that God will not even entrust our thoughts with it. Oh, what a great blessing is this state in which that accursed one can do us no harm! Great are the gains which come to the soul with God working in it and neither we ourselves nor anyone else hindering Him. What will He not give Who so much loves giving and can give all that He will?[392]

To live in the Will of God does not imply that one has vanquished the malignant foe once and for all. One must be vigilant because "the devil needs only see an open door in order to rain down upon us thousands of ills."[393]

Self-Defense

"All we have mentioned here takes place passively without one's doing or undoing anything."[394] In other words, the soul has been provoked, obliged to undergo the horrors and assaults of the Evil One to varying degrees. The person has not sought this.

To think that St. John of the Cross means by "reaction," that a soul, now in a state of transforming union, becomes the aggressor would be to misunderstand him. Engagement in spiritual combat and vanquishing the last of the seven heads has nothing to do with revenge against the devil or self-vindication. Spiritual combat, "reacting", according to Sanjuanistic doctrine will always take the form of simple self-defense.

With this in mind, it makes sense to understand what is to be done to best defend oneself in this phase, according to the teaching of the Mystical Doctor. We will consider two dominant themes: behavior and final success as a result of this behavior.

Behavior: The joy-filled state of transforming union ought not to be understood in terms of a "means" to something yet beyond it. Nonetheless, there are means to be used in order to protect this state.

The means that the Mystical Doctor offers us include an attitude to be adopted which has absolute trust in our Lord's victory, yet it implies a marked defensiveness. In order to avoid the ambushes set by the enemy, the soul must take to the narrow road, when leaving its house following these Sanjuanistic indications: it should travel by night,[395] be well camouflaged or "disguised",[396] and be well accompanied.[397]

Certainly, the limits of this small book do not permit me to elaborate on these aspects with the depth they merit. I will have to settle for a glance at these elements, inspired by St. John's teaching.

Travelling by Night: Darkness, rather than a thing in itself, is a privation of light. This is the term our author uses for self-denial, a privation of likes and tastes in everything:

We here describe as night the privation of every kind of pleasure which belongs to the desire; for, even as night is naught but the privation of light, and, consequently, of all objects that can be seen by means of light, whereby the visual faculty remains unoccupied[83] and in darkness, even so likewise the mortification of desire may be called night to the soul. For, when the soul is deprived of the pleasure of its desire in all things, it remains, as it were, unoccupied and in darkness. For even as the visual faculty, by means of light, is nourished and fed by objects which can be seen, and which, when the light is quenched, are not seen, even so, by means of the desire, the soul is nourished and fed by all things wherein it can take pleasure according to its faculties; and, when this also is quenched, or rather, mortified, the soul ceases to feed upon the pleasure of all things, and thus, with respect to its desire, it remains unoccupied and in darkness.[398]

Deprivation of tastes and appetites, renunciation is night: "in the dark and with nothing."[399] Thomas says something similar: "The creature is darkness in comparison with the excellence of the Divine light; and therefore, the creature's knowledge in its own nature is called "evening" knowledge.[400]

Active mortification must be exercised in order to develop true detachment of heart from created things. In this way, the soul manages to "banish the devil" for a time.[401] The devil has a certain power and ability to attack the soul – not only in itself, but also in the things it uses or those things around it.[402] He will especially pay attention to the affections, desires, and likes where Satan will torment the person, obscure his vision, in hopes of sullying and weakening the soul.[403]

With that in mind, detaching oneself from ones likes and purifying one's affections, the devil is disarmed in that regard. To travel by night means to mortify oneself and, in that way, the soul defends itself from certain wiles and deceits of the Evil One.

Camouflage and Armor: There are two types of battle we are engaged in: one active, the other passive. The active fight is, in the strict sense, combat with the enemy of our souls. The passive battle regards the passive purification of the senses and the spirit. This purification, desired by God, is a prerequisite for union with Him. Such a fight is carried out defensively and offensively if one is to arrive to the celestial homeland.

To better understand this symmetric relationship between the particular temptations and the corresponding weapons, St. John divides them according to the type of fight in which the souls finds itself: active or passive.

The disguise St. John of the Cross suggests is a three-piece habit which covers the soul, hiding it from the intrusive eyes of the enemy. Dressing up the soul in this way reorients it towards the divine Spouse and makes it pleasing to him. It also serves as a protection, allowing the soul to carry out its tasks unhindered.[404] The soul progressing in grace must continuously face its three enemies: the world, the flesh, and the devil.

> The soul, then, touched with the love of Christ the Spouse, and longing to attain to His grace and gain His goodwill, goes forth here disguised with that disguise which most vividly represents the affections of its spirit and which will protect it most securely on its journey from its adversaries and enemies, which are the devil, the world and the flesh. Thus the livery which it wears is of three chief colours—white, green and purple—denoting the three theological virtues, faith, hope and charity. By these the soul will not only gain the grace and goodwill of its Beloved, but it will travel in security and complete protection from its three enemies: for faith is an inward tunic of a whiteness so pure that it completely dazzles the eyes of the understanding.[405]

With regard to the active battle, the soul, dressed in this fashion, finds "total security against the wiles of the devil."[406] "More than all the other virtues,"[407] it is faith that most directly and efficiently preserves the soul in its contemplative activity, protecting it from insidious attacks. In similar terms, St. Peter counsels faith against the attacks of the devil: *Stand up to him strong in the faith.*[408]

Faith is an inner tunic of such pure whiteness that it blinds the sight of every intellect. When the soul is clothed in faith the devil is ignorant of how to hinder her, neither is he successful in his efforts, for faith gives her strong protection - more than do all the other virtues - against the devil, who is the mightiest and most astute enemy.[409]

St. John of the Cross calls faith a "dark ray,"[410] and in relation to the devil, the light of faith is darker than dark.[411] And thus the soul that journeys through this night, we may say, journeys in concealment and in hiding from the devil, as will be more clearly seen hereafter. Wherefore the soul says that it went forth 'in darkness and secure'; for one that has such happiness as to be able to journey through the darkness of faith, taking faith for his guide, like to one that is blind, and leaving behind all natural imaginings and spiritual reasonings, journeys very securely.[412]

With regard to the passive battle the soul finds itself engaged in, St. John of the Cross tells us that simple knowing through faith supersedes all forms, figures, imaginings, and ridding itself of all of these natural phantasms and reasonings.[413] Therefore, "the less the soul works through its own powers, the mores securely it advances, because it walks by faith."[414]

It is not enough to go out by night. One must immerse oneself in the darkness, travelling in the dense obscurity of faith.[415] "Faith darkens the intellect and deprives it of all its natural abilities, thus allowing it to be united with divine Wisdom."[416]

Beyond the senses, the soul must blind its rational part in order to allow itself to be guided. One must abandon the familiar avenues of reason and sense (always woefully limited) and be led like a blind man: courageously taking to the incomprehensible path of God:

> Wherefore, upon this road, to enter upon the road is to leave the
> road; or, to express it better, it is to pass on to the goal and to leave
> one's own way, and to enter upon that which has no way, which
> is God. For the soul that attains to this state has no longer any
> ways or methods, still less is it attached to ways and methods, or
> is capable of being attached to them. I mean ways of
> understanding, or of perception, or of feeling…. it enters within
> the limits of the supernatural, which has no way, yet in substance
> has all ways.[417]

The active battle against the spirit of the world engages the virtue
of hope: "Dressed in the green garment of hope, the soul stands sure
against its second enemy, the world."[418]

On the other hand, the virtue of hope purifies the faculty of the
memory:

> Hope voids and withdraws the memory from all creature
> possessions; for, as Saint Paul says, *hope is for that which is not
> possessed* (Rom 8:24-25) and thus it withdraws the memory from
> that which it is capable of possessing and sets it on that for which
> it hopes. And for this cause hope in God alone prepares the
> memory purely for union with God.[419]

Charity is the weapon engaged in battle against the flesh, for it
invigorates the other virtues:

> This cloak of charity, causes greater love in the Beloved, not only
> protects the soul and hides it from the third enemy, which is the
> flesh (for where there is true love of God there enters neither love

of self nor that of the things of self), but even gives worth to the other virtues, bestowing on them vigor and strength to protect the soul, and grace and beauty to please the Beloved with them, for without charity no virtue has grace before God.

Meanwhile, charity's role in the passive battle is as follows:

Charity, in the same way, voids and annihilates the affections and desires of the will for whatever is not God, and sets them upon Him alone; and thus this virtue prepares this faculty and unites it with God through love. And thus, since the function of these virtues is the withdrawal of the soul from all that is less than God, their function is consequently that of joining it with God.[420]

The Shield of Faith Protects Us from the Devil

Finally, draw your strength from the Lord and from his mighty power. Put on the armor of God so that you may be able to stand firm against the tactics of the devil. For our struggle is not with flesh and blood but with the principalities, with the powers, with the world rulers of this present darkness, with the evil spirits in the heavens. Therefore, put on the armor of God, that you may be able to resist on the evil day and, having done everything, to hold your ground. So stand fast with your loins girded in truth, clothed with righteousness as a breastplate-and your feet shod in readiness for the gospel of peace. In all circumstances, hold faith as a shield, to quench all [the] flaming arrows of the evil one. And take the helmet of salvation and the sword of the Spirit, which is the word of God (Eph 6:10-17).

St. John of the Cross states clearly that his purpose is not to lay out rules for discerning which supernatural phenomena are of God and which are demonic falsifications. Nonetheless, guiding principles are to be found in his doctrine.

> I say, then, that with regard to all these imaginary visions and apprehensions and to all other forms and species whatsoever, which present themselves beneath some particular kind of knowledge or image or form, whether they be false and come from the devil or are recognized as true and coming from God, the understanding must not be embarrassed by them or feed upon them, neither must the soul desire to receive them or to have them, lest it should no longer be detached, free, pure and simple, without any mode or manner, as is required for union.[421]

The Mystical Doctor invites the contemplative soul to distinguish between essentials and accidentals, giving faith primacy above all other communications, considerations, and images – even those that have a divine source. Does St. John mean willful rejection of divinely inspired communications?

It is always well, then, that the soul should reject these things, and close its eyes to them, regardless of their source. For, unless it does so, it will prepare the way for those things that come from the devil, and will give him such influence that, not only will his visions come in place of God's, but his visions will begin to increase, and those of God to cease, in such manner that the devil will have all the power and God will have none.

So it has happened to many incautious and ignorant souls, who rely on these things to such an extent that many of them have found it hard to return to God in purity of faith; and many have been unable to return, so securely has the devil rooted himself in them; for which reason it is well to resist and reject them all.

For, by the rejection of evil visions, the errors of the devil are avoided, and by the rejection of good visions no hindrance is offered to faith and the spirit harvests the fruit of them. And just as, when the soul allows them entrance, God begins to withhold them because the soul is becoming attached to them and is not profiting by them as it should, while the devil insinuates and increases his own visions, where he finds occasion and cause for them; just so, when the soul is resigned, or even averse to them, the devil begins to desist, since he sees that he is working it no harm; and contrariwise God begins to increase and magnify His favours in a soul that is so humble and detached, making it ruler over many things, even as He made the servant who was faithful in small things.[422]

The Mystical Doctor, while not having a negative view of possible divine communications, certainly counsels a negative reaction to them. Such an attitude will not offend God in the slightest, since he knows that the prudent person does this out of love and a sense of protection of one's own spiritual life.

St. John's reaction to corporeal visions is practical:

"…(H)ence it follows that the soul must be pure and simple, neither bounded by, nor attached to, any particular kind of intelligence, nor modified by any limitation of form, species and image. As God comes not within any image or form, neither is contained within any particular kind of intelligence, so the soul, in order to reach God, must likewise come within no distinct form or kind of intelligence.[423]

God is not an experience and cannot be contained in one. By way of pure theological virtue the soul actually touches God and enters into union with him. Visions and other similar experiences do not offer the same security that faith affords the soul.

One's reaction to these phenomena ought to be to close one's eyes to them,[424] without entertaining any desire to examine the source of experience.[425] Elsewhere he counsels not admitting them or giving them any credit or attention,[426] since to admit them is tantamount to opening the door to the Evil One and his deceits and other similar things.[427]

Regarding imaginary visions, we are counseled to react in similar terms: suspicion, rejection, letting them die of neglect; since these will always be limited, yet the wisdom of God – to which the intellect must be united – is not subject to the same limitations as human cognition which deals with particulars,[428] and, as a result, is an insufficient and disproportionate means for such matters.[429]

With regard to spiritual communications, one should neither desire nor seek them.[430]

> A pure and simple soul knows to remain circumspect and humble in these matters and ought to energetically resist them, And if it is true that, for the reasons already described, it behooves the soul to close its eyes to the aforementioned revelations which come to it, and which concern the propositions of the faith, how much more necessary will it be neither to receive nor to give credit to other revelations relating to different things, wherein the devil habitually meddles so freely that I believe it impossible for a man not to be deceived in many of them unless he strive to reject them, such an appearance of truth and security does the devil give them[431]

Such spiritual communications are not necessary to love God wholly and the desire for them can actually be a hindrance to pure love of God.[432]

At this point it ought not shock us that St. John of the Cross counsels similar behavior with regard to spiritual visions that represent creatures.[433] Such knowledge as this, whether it be of God or not, can be of very little assistance to the progress of the soul on its journey to God if the soul desire it and be attached to it; on the contrary, if it were not scrupulous in rejecting it, not only would it be hindered on its road, but it would even be greatly harmed and led far astray.[434]

If the soul remains strong in its resolve, humbly rejecting such communications, the devil, upon noticing that he cannot deceive this person, will attempt to sully that person's naked faith and poverty of spirit.[435]

Regarding revelations, one should "take great care to reject them,"[436] rather, with eyes closed, support himself in the Church's doctrine and the darkness of faith.[437]

Locutions ought to receive the same treatment since they can harm the faith.[438] And let it be carefully noted that a soul should never act according to its own opinion or accept anything of what these locutions express, without much reflection and without taking advice of another. For strange and subtle deceptions may arise in this matter; so much so that I myself believe that the soul that does not set itself against accepting such things cannot fail to be deceived by many of them.[439]

Finally, regarding interior sentiments, one ought not seek them out nor desire them. Otherwise, such a predisposition can prepare oneself for disaster. The devil is a master at taking advantage of these situations and presenting his counterfeits when the dispositions are there – especially using the sentiments or anything that might lull the soul into abandoning itself to his notions.[440]

Being well accompanied

By this our author means that we ought not trust ourselves too much, but rather recognize our indigence and benefit from the counsel of others. This requires humility, stripping oneself of whatever self-sufficiency and arrogance or presumption one might have. Of such souls, St. John says:

> Yet these humble souls, far from desiring to be anyone's teacher, are ready to take a road different from the one they are following, if told to do so. For they do not believe they could ever be right themselves. They rejoice when others receive praise, and their only sorrow is that they do not serve God as these others do.[441]

> A soul that must overcome the devil's strength will be unable to do so without prayer, nor will it be able to understand his deceits without mortification and humility.[442]

Not only is humility a requirement for a relationship with God, it protects the soul from the devil's onslaughts. Lacking this foundational virtue the would-be contemplative opens himself up to the devil's thousand lies.[443] And this humility, in order to be authentic, must have body and soul, words and deeds – a true humility of heart without which one can not repel demons.[444]

St. Teresa, for her part, speaks of this humility as absolute trust in the Lord which grants her new-found strength:

> Seeing, then, that our Lord is so powerful, - as I see and know He is, — and that the evil spirits are His slaves, of which there can be no doubt, because it is of faith, - and I a servant of this our Lord and King, - what harm can Satan do unto me? Why have I not strength enough to fight against all hell? I took up the cross in my hand, -I was changed in a moment into another person, and it seemed as if God had really given me courage enough not to be

afraid of encountering all the evil spirits. It seemed to me that I could, with the cross, easily defeat them altogether. So I cried out, Come on, all of you; I am the servant of our Lord: I should like to see what you can do against me.

And certainly, they seemed to be afraid of me, for I was left in peace: I feared them so little, that the terrors, which until now oppressed me, quitted me altogether; and though I saw them occasionally, - I was never again afraid of them - on the contrary, they seemed to be afraid of me. I found myself endowed with a certain authority over them, given me by the Lord of all, so that I cared no more for them than for flies. They seem to be such cowards; for their strength fails them at the sight of any one who despises them. These enemies have not the courage to assail any but those whom they see ready to give in to them, or when God permits them to do so, for the greater good of His servants, whom they may try and torment.[445]

Nonetheless, confronting the Evil One ought to be directed by prudence. This virtue permits us to use the weapons provided by the Lord to good effect. For St. Teresa, these are: prayer and "carrying one's cross." Contemplatives are professional cross-bearers:

Contemplatives need to carry the banner of humility, bearing with all the blows that come their way, without responding in kind. Their task is that of suffering like Christ, carrying the cross high.[446]

And the cross is the best of weapons to defeat the devil. "Be stout-hearted... make the brave decision, knowing that you will battle every demon, but with the best weapon: the cross."[447]

The great source of our deliverance from the cunning devices and the sweetness which Satan sends is to begin with a resolution to walk in the way of the Cross from the very first, and not to desire any sweetness at all, seeing that our Lord Himself has pointed out to us the way of perfection, saying, *Take up thy cross and follow Me.* He is our example; and whosoever follows His counsels only to please Him has nothing to fear. In the improvement which they detect in themselves, they who do so will see that this is no work of Satan and if they fall, they have a sign of the presence of our Lord in their rising again at once.[448]

This hand-to-hand combat with the evil imagery is not original to St. Teresa. St. Paul speaks of the sword of the Spirit. This weapon is what wins the day on the field of battle. Of course, the sword is the Cross of Christ. And, according to St. Teresa, our shield is adorned with the heraldry of the five wounds of Christ.[449]

Unlike St. John of the Cross, St. Teresa speaks several times of the efficacy of holy water in spiritual combat.

I know by frequent experience that there is nothing which puts the devils to flight like holy water. They run away before the sign of the cross also, but they return immediately: great, then, must be the power of holy water. As for me, my soul is conscious of a special and most distinct consolation whenever I take it. Indeed, I feel almost always a certain refreshing, which I cannot describe, together with an inward joy, which comforts my whole soul. This is no fancy, nor a thing which has occurred once only; for it has happened very often, and I have watched it very carefully. I may compare what I feel with that which happens to a person in great heat, and very thirsty, drinking a cup of cold water—his whole being is refreshed. I consider that everything ordained by the

Church is very important; and I have a joy in reflecting that the words of the Church are so mighty, that they endow water with power, so that there shall be so great a difference between holy water and water that has never been blessed.[450]

Angels

An aspect of this humility St. John alludes to is the necessary dependence on others for spiritual perfection as we have seen. St. John does not only include other men in his list of means but also refers to the work of angels in the order of our salvation and perfection. The angels can communicate what they contemplate already in heaven, while men of virtue (confessors and spiritual directors) can transmit their counsel and common desire for the divine Spouse.[451] The angels instruct us interiorly, while people provide us with exterior aid.[452]

Angels are our mediators. Not only do they present our supplications to the Lord, they also bestow upon us God's favor and blessings; guiding us, as good shepherds by way of their sweet communications and divine inspirations.[453] Like the Good Shepherd, these heavenly friends protect us from prowling wolves, so says St. John of the Cross.[454]

As a result, if one desires to approach God unimpeded in his exercise of divine love, it is enough to have recourse to angels with a simple invocation.[455] They are delighted to oblige since it is their God given mission.[456]

Men

Proper to a humble soul is to not hazard along the ways of God alone. Anyone serious about advancing in the spiritual life has recourse to men of counsel.[457] God has ordained it that men should be aided by other men on the path towards configuration with

Christ.[458] This serves as an objective standard in a field which often suffers from so much subjectivism. Allow oneself to be guided, strict spiritual dependence on a spiritual director protects the individual from his own caprices and subjectivist interpretations of his own experience. St. John of the Cross calls humility the weapon which most directly strikes the enemy.[459] Humility is usually best attained through prayer, confident appeals to Christ, in submission, and obedience.

> "Let, then, the first precaution be that, without the command of obedience, you never take upon yourself any work -- apart from the obligations of your state -- however good and full of charity it may seem, whether for yourself or for anyone else inside or outside the house. By such a practice you will win merit and security, avoid possession, and flee from harm and evils unknown to you."[460]

Holding to these counsels will prove a consolation and support – especially when the advanced soul experiences supernatural communications. The Lord, says the Mystical Doctor, does not want individuals to judge for themselves what comes from God and what does not, much less to conform oneself with the content of such messages, without seeking the Church's judgment and speaking with her ministers.[461]

When transmitting such things to one's spiritual director or confessor, St. John counsels speaking with clarity, integrity, and simplicity.[462] This spiritual father ought to be mature, experienced, wise, and discreet,[463] and the aspirant ought to obey his counsel.[464]

An attitude such makes for a fruitful exercise of humility. Our author writes: "for the sake of the humility and submission and mortification of the soul, it is well to relate everything to the director, even though he makes no account of it all and consider it of no importance."[465]

Not only does the contemplative exercise – and therefore maintain his humility – he will be richly blessed for it:

> For although there may seem no reason to speak of it, or to spend time upon doing so, since the soul is acting safely, as we have said, if it rejects it and neither pays heed to it nor desires it -- especially if it be a question of visions or revelations or other supernatural communications, which are either quite clear or very nearly so -- nevertheless, it is very necessary to give an account of all these, although it may seem to the soul that there is no reason for so doing.
>
> And this for three causes. First, because, as we have said, God communicates many things, the effect, power, light and certainty.[466]

To travel by night, to go about disguised, and to be well accompanied in obedience – these are other words for mortification and self-denial of the senses, the theological virtues in the spirit, and humility in everything. These are the three aspects the Mystical Doctor lays out for us on how to react to the attacks of the Evil One. Following his counsel brings about spiritual freedom.

Final Victory

The attitudes and behavior that the Mystical Doctor counsels above are failsafe. Obedience to them will ensure that the soul not fall prey to the devil's traps. On the other hand, the above-mentioned attitudes and behaviors have a much broader reaching effect than mere defense against the adversary. They move the soul along towards transforming union.

The truly generous soul will not go unrecompensed by the Lord. And Christ will not be outdone in generosity. "If the soul seeks out God, much more does God seek that soul."[467] To achieve spiritual marriage has as a contingency the absolute route and humiliation of the devil. After many struggles and much generosity in spiritual exercises in which the devil worked hard but to no avail, he must finally admit defeat,[468] and is cast far from that soul.[469] The contemplative soul remains victorious[470] and <u>immune</u> to further attacks of the Evil One. He has become <u>formidable</u> to his opponent and rests in the <u>peace and joy</u> of Christ.

Immunity from attack: The soul which has given itself totally to God, "with a certain consummation of loving union,"[471] harbors no more appetites, nor images, forms, or affections for created things. This pristine soul has been purified of everything that is not God.[472] Its virtues have been developed to such a high degree that one cannot see daylight between them: they form an integral whole – nothing missing. This is the *honestia* St. Thomas speaks of in which the truly virtuous person is virtuous in everything and at all times. There is an integrity that is complete and virtue is not lop-sided.[473] And such a person is not moved by the flesh, the devil, or the world's trifles.[474]

Finally, the "watching fears of night" do not reach her, for she is now so clearly illumined and strong and rests so firmly in her God that the devils can neither cause her obscurity through their darknesses, nor frighten her with their terrors, nor awaken her by their attacks. Nothing can reach or molest her now that she has withdrawn from all things and entered into her God where she enjoys all peace, tastes all sweetness, and delights in all delights insofar as this earthly state allows.[475]

Formidable adversary: The transformed soul has "become God by participation inasmuch as this is possible in this life."[476] As a result, it receives some of God's properties,[477] in its weakness God's strength is freed up to manifest itself,[478] striking terror into the enemy.[479]

After spiritually purified souls reach the state of perfect union with God through love in the "seventh mansion," the diabolic temptations are over, and demons are afraid of them. "Nor did Aminadab appear," John says in the end of the Spiritual Canticle. Aminadab symbolizes the devil, and in this state the soul is so favored, so strong and victorious that the devil knows he has lost the battle. At this stage, the devil flees in immense fear and does not venture to reappear. Teresa, also victorious, perceived that the devil was terrified of her, but not she of the devil: "[Devils] seem to be afraid of me. I have acquired an authority over them, bestowed upon me by the Lord of all, so that they are no more trouble to me; now they fly" (Life 242).

In this state, souls are transformed in God. They are divine by participation and possess Christ-like qualities. In them the Redeemer has defeated Satan and his kingdom of darkness. Teresa and John of the Cross struggled with demons, but in the end their victory — and God's — was complete.[480]

Demons do not dare attack a soul in this state, nor even hazard to approach such a one as this on account of their fear, confused by the soul's brilliance and strength. They fear this person as they fear God.[481]

Peace and Joy: Peace follows the victorious combat.[482] The soul is invested with peace and experiences it throughout its entire being,[483] so much so that that the entire spiritual edifice appears to have been built up by peace.[484]

The house and all its inhabitants (the senses) is in perfect order[485] and the intellective aspect is "inundated by a river of peace."[486] During the spiritual betrothal the upper and more spiritual parts of the soul were stilled; now the entire being with all of its senses, powers, and faculties experience perfect quiet. The consummation of spiritual marriage has put a stop to every sort of attack.[487]

This, says St. John of the Cross, is the return to original righteousness.[488] This soul is confirmed in grace.[489] This is an immense joy that penetrates every fiber of one's being: a glorious delight.[490] Within the deepest part of the soul's intimacy a wedding feast is being celebrated and the Holy Spirit has brought all of his fruits.[491]

Unable to contain itself anymore, the soul breaks out into song. A song of victory, peace, and joy:

> One dark night, fired with love's urgent
> Longings- ah, the sheer grace! -
> I went out unseen,
> My house being now all stilled.
>
> O guiding night!
> O night more lovely than the dawn!
> O night that has united
> The Lover with his beloved,
> Transforming the beloved in her Lover

Endnotes

[1] A 2, 11, 10.

[2] *Dizionario di Mistica,* Luigi Borrielo,*et. al. Editrice Vaticana,* Citta Vaticana, 2000.

[3] D 1, 8,2.

[4] A 2, 16,9.

[5] LF 2,9.

[6] LF 1,4.

[7] A 2, 15,5.

[8] *Idem.*

[9] SC 11,3.

[10] SC 1,1.

[11] Romance 4.

[12] Romance 9.

[13] SC 23, 6.

[14] A 1, 13.

[15] SC 31, 2.

[16] LF 3, 46.

[17] A, 1, 13

[18] A 2, 7.

[19] A 2,2,2.

[20] SC 22-23.

[21] A, 2, 9.

[22] LF 1, 11.

[23] SC 11,11.

[24] SC 8, 3.

[25] SC 39, 7.

[26] Canon 395.

[27] A 2, chpt 26, 17.

[28] *Relación de la M. Ana d San Alberto.* Ap. Silv. IV, p. 399.

[29] Bruno, *op. cit.* P. 130.

[30] *Letter* 210.

[31] *Obras del Venerable Fray Juan de la Cruz,* Vol IV, p. 378.

[32] Loc. Cit, Vol. V, p. 380.

33 *Letter* 48.
34 *Letter* 269.
35 Obras de San Juan de la Cruz, Vol V,
36 C 3,6.
37 *Cautelas* 2.
38 *Cautelas* 3.
39 A 1.4,4.
40 A 1. 4,8.
41 C 3,7.
42 *Precautions* 5.
43 *Ibid,* 7.
44 *Ibid* 8-9.
45 A, Preface.
46 D 1, 13, chap. 13.
47 D 1. 13, 3.
48 A 1, 8, 3.
49 C 5,1.
50 C 4,1;
51 C 7,1; D 1.2, chap. 12,4.
52 A 1.2, chap. 8,3.
53 *S. Th.* I, q. 63, a. 3,c.
54 A 1.2, chp.11,1.
55 D 1.2, chap. 23,8.
56 A 1.1, chap. 2,2.
57 D 1.1, chap. 14,1.
58 C 3, 11.
59 A 2, 11, 10.
60 *S. Th.* I, q. 96, a.1,5; A 1.2, chap. 21,7.
61 A 2, 21, 7.
62 A 1. 2, chap. 21, 11; Loc. Cit. 8.
63 A 2, 21, 8.
64 A 2, 21, 9-10.
65 A 1.2, chap.26, 14.
66 *S. Th.* 1, q. 57, a.4,c.

[67] *S. Th.* 1, 64, a.1, ad 5.

[68] A 1. 2, chap. 21, 9.

[69] *Ibid.*

[70] *Loc. Cit.* 11.

[71] *Loc. Cit.* 7. Thomas agrees: "In causes effects are seen; and in effects, their causes." *S. Th.* I, q. 58, a. 3, ad 2.

[72] A 1.2, chap. 21, 8. See also *S. Th.* I 1.58, a.3, ad 2.

[73] *A Loc. Cit.* 7; Loc. Cit. 10.

[74] *S Th.* I, q. 14, a. 13.

[75] A 1.2, chap. 21, 7.

[76] A 1, 1,1.

[77] D 1.2, chap. 23, 6.

[78] *Loc. Cit.* 8.

[79] *Loc. Cit.* 4; L 4, 16.

[80] D 1 17, 1.

[81] D 1.23, 11-12.

[82] L 4,14.

[83] D 1.2,chap.23,11. A 1.3, chap. 22,6.

[84] *S Th.* I, q. 63, a. 3,c .

[85] D 1.2, chap. 23, 8; C A, 25,2; A 1.3, chap. 15,3; A 1.3, chap. 37,1.; C B, chap. 16,3.

[86] SC B,3, 10.

[87] *Cfr.* Mark 3:27.

[88] A 1.19, 8.

[89] SC A, 39, 3; C B, 40,3.

[90] A 1, 26,7.

[91] *Cautelas*, 9.

[92] *Ibid.*

[93] Job, 41:24.

[94] SC B, 3,9.

[95] SC A, 3, 8.

[96] SC A, 3,1.

[97] SC A 3, 9; SC B, 3,10.

[98] SC, 3,9.

[99] *S. Th.* I, *q.* 114, *a.* 2.
[100] A 3, 31, 4-5.
[101] A 2, 12,3.
[102] In Spanish, as in most languages with gendered nouns, "soul" is feminine.
[103] SC, Commentary, 11,4.
[104] *Romance* II.
[105] *Life,* 24, 10.
[106] *S. Th. II-IIae, Q.* 80, *a.* 3, *ad* 1.
[107] *Way,* 25.
[108] *ACM,* 2, 15.
[109] *Opusc. LXV.*
[110] *De Veritate, q.* xviii, *a.* 1; *Contra Gent.,* III, ch. Li.
[111] *Life,* xiv.
[112] *Ibid.*
[113] *Way,* ch. Xxx.
[114] *Fifth Mansion,* ch 1.
[115] *Life,* no. 40.
[116] *Treatise on the Love of God,* bk. Vi, ch. ix.
[117] *First Letter to Fr. Rodrigo Alvarez.*
[118] *Life,* No. 275. Appendix
[119] *In div. nomin.,* ch. vii, 4.
[120] *S Th,* I-II q 69, a.2 ad 3.
[121] *Via compendia ad Deum,* c 9, n.4.
[122] A 2, 13.
[123] St. Teresa also speaks of this difficulty with the wandering imagination in the Fourth Mansion.
[124] *Fifth Mansion.*
[125] A 2, 15, 2.
[126] Rom 8:35-39.
[127] *S Th.* II-II q. 180, a 8, ad 2.
[128] *Life,* chpt.4 & 18.
[129] *S Th.* I q. 109, a.3.
[130] *S. Th,* I, 111, *a.* 3.
[131] A 2, 29.

[132] A, 2, chp. 24.

[133] A, 2, chpt. 23, 3.

[134] *De inquisition pacis,* Bk V, part III, ch. Xii.

[135] A 2, 29, 10.

[136] A 3, 31, 4-5.

[137] L 3, 64.

[138] See A 2, 11, 5-8.

[139] A 2, 11, 5-8.

[140] *Idem.*

[141] DN 2, 23, 6.

[142] DN 2, 23,7.

[143] *Loc. Cit.* 6.

[144] *Idem.*

[145] *S. Th.* I, *q.* 114, *a.* 1, *ad* 3.

[146] DN 2, 23, 10.

[147] A 3, 43, 1.

[148] A 3, 43, 3.

[149] *Loc. Cit.* 3.

[150] *Loc. Cit.* 13.

[151] *Loc. Cit.* 12

[152] *Loc. Cit.* 21.

[153] SC 16, 9.

[154] L 1, 9.

[155] DN 2, 17, 2.

[156] A 2, 31, 2.

[157] A 3, 4,1.

[158] D 2, chpt.23, 2.

[159] A 2, 21, 11-13.

[160] DN 2, chpt. 16, 2; A 2, chpt. 11, 8.

[161] A 2, chpt. 11,5; *S. Th.* Q. 111, *a.* 4

[162] A 3, chpt. 4, 1.

[163] *Idem.*

[164] A 3, chpt. 3, 6.

[165] DN 1, chpt. 4, 2; 2, chpt. 2, 3.

166 A 2, chpt. 16, 3.

167 DN 1, chpt. 4, 3.

168 A 3, chpt 37, 1.

169 A 2, chpt. 12, 2.

170 DN 2, chpt. 23, 8.

171 A 2, 10, 1. Further, Aquinas says that "man's intellect is moved by an angel, on the part of the object, which by the power of the angelic light is proposed to man's knowledge. And in this way the will also can be moved by a creature from without…" *S. Th. I-IIae, q* 9, *a.* 6 c.

172 Moreno, p. 266-267.

173 A 2, chpt. 23, 4.

174 Loc. Cit. 4.

175 DN 2, chpt. 2, 2.

176 A 2, chpt. 26, 17; A 3, chpt. 6, 2.

177 DN 2, chpt. 2, 3.

178 A 2, chpt. 26, 17; A 3, chpt. 10, 1.

179 A 2, chpt. 27, 17.

180 A 2, chpt. 24, 7.

181 A 2, 26, 14.

182 Loc. Cit. 17.

183 *Ibid.*

184 A 2, chpt. 29, 11.

185 *Ibid.*

186 A 2, chpt. 29, 11.

187 A 3 chpt. 27, 1.

188 A 3 chpt. 29, 1.

189 A 3, chpt. 37, 1.

190 DN 2, chpt. 4, 3.

191 A 2 chpt. 11, 6. See also *S. Th.* I, *q.* 111, *a.* 2.*c.*

192 DN 2, chpt. 2, 2;

193 A 2, chpt. 26, 17.

194 A 3, chpt. 4, 1.

195 A 3, chpt. 10, 1.

196 C B, chpt. 40, 3; chpt 16, 7; A 2, chpt. 11, 10; C

197 A 2, chpt. 11, 10.

198 A 3, chpt. 24, 1.

199 A 2, chpt. 11, 1; 3, chpt. 24, 1.

200 *Loc. Cit.* 10.

201 *Ibid.*

202 A 2, chpt. 23, 4; 3, chpt. 4, 1.

203 A 2, chpt 29, 10.

204 A 3, chpt. 4, 1.

205 A 2, chpt. 26, 17.

206 A 2, chpt. 29, 10.

207 *Ibid.*

208 A 3, chpt. 4, 1.

209 L 3, 63.

210 C 16, 9.

211 A 3, chpt. 6, 2.

212 A 2, chpt. 11, 6.

213 C 16, 6; 20-21, 9.

214 C 20-21, 9; A 2, chpt. 11, 6.

215 DN 1, chpt. 14, 3; L 3, 64.

216 DN 2, 23, 5; loc. Cit. 8; C 20-21, 15.

217 L 3, 64.

218 A 2, chpt. 23, 4; 2, chpt. 11, 3.

219 *S. Th. I-IIae, q. 80, a. 2. C.*

220 A 3, chpt. 4, 1.

221 *Ibid.*

222 *Loc. Cit.* 2.

223 D 1, chpt. 13, 14.

224 *Loc. Cit.* 11.

225 *El engaño.*

226 A 2, chpt. 11, 7.

227 A 3, chpt. 11, 1.

228 A 2, chpt. 11, 7.

229 A 2, chpt.26, 5.

230 A 2, chpt. 11, 12.

[231] A 2, chpt. 27, 4.

[232] A 3, chpt. 10, 2.

[233] *Ibid.*

[234] A 2, chpt. 26, 6,

[235] Our author uses the term "ape." *Ibid.*

[236] A 2, chpt. 11, 7.

[237] A 2, chpt. 16, 3.

[238] A 2, chpt. 27, 17; 29, 10; 27, 17.

[239] St. John of the Cross uses the word *astucia* frequently

[240] L 3, 63, 64.

[241] A 3, chpt. 37, 1.

[242] A 3, chpt. 10, 1.

[243] *Ibid.*

[244] *S. Th.* I, *q.* 64, *a.* 2 *ad* 5.

[245] A 2, chpt. 29, 11.

[246] A 2, chpt. 30, 4.

[247] A 2. Chpt. 31, 2.

[248] *S. Th.* III *q.* 41, *a.* 4.

[249] *S. Th.* III *q.* 8, *a.* 7, *ad* 2.

[250] A 2, chpt. 31, 2.

[251] *S. Th.* III, *q.* 41, *a.* 1, *ad* 3.

[252] A 2, chpt. 24, 7.

[253] *S. Th.* III *q.* 41, *a.*2, 3.

[254] A 2, chpt. 29, 1o

[255] D 2, chpt. 2, 3.

[256] A 3, chpt. 10, 2

[257] A 2, chpt. 29, 10.

[258] A 2, chpt. 11, 10.

[259] *Ibid.*

[260] DN 1, chpt. 1, 2.

[261] "Ignorant children" says our author. A 1, chpt. 4, 5.

[262] DN 1, chpt. 1, 3.

[263] DN 1, chpt. 6, 6.

[264] DN 1, chpt. 1, 3.

[265] This is a common theme with our author: A 2, chpt. 27, 6; A 3, chpt. 6, 2; A 3, chpt. 29, 1; DN 1, chpt. 14, 1; C 3, 8; C 3,9, *etc.*

[266] *Loc. Cit.* 2.

[267] *Loc. Cit.* 3.

[268] *Ibid.*

[269] DN 1, chpt. 4, 1.

[270] DN 1, chpt. 3.

[271] DN 1, chpt. 6, 1.

[272] *Ibid.*

[273] *Loc. Cit.* 2

[274] *Ibid.*

[275] DN 1, chpt. 4, 3.

[276] A 2, chpt. 14.1.

[277] DN 1, chpt. 8, 3.

[278] *Ibid.*

[279] DN 1, chpt. 14, 6.

[280] DN 1, chpt. 13, 1; loc. Cit. 4.

[281] DN 1, chpt. 14, 1.

[282] *Loc. Cit.* 2.

[283] *Loc. Cit.* 3.

[284] *Life,* 13,1.

[285] *Ibid.,* 11,4.

[286] *Ibid.,* 8,7.

[287] *Ibid.,* 13,8, 9.

[288] *First Mansion,* 2, 11.

[289] *Reflections on the Love of God,* 2,3.

[290] *S Th.* I, *q.* 114, *a.*3.

[291] *Life,* 136, 8.

[292] *Reflections,* 2,1.

[293] *Ibid.,* 2, 14.

[294] *Way of Perfection,* 38, 1.

[295] *Ibid.,* 38, 2.

[296] *Second Mansions,* 1,3.

[297] DN 1, chpt. 10, 2.

[298] DN 1, chpt. 14, 1.
[299] DN 2, chpt. 1, 1.
[300] C 22, 3.
[301] Moreno, P. 265.
[302] C 16, 2.
[303] A 2, chpt. 11,1.; A 2, chpt. 17, 4.
[304] DN 2, chpt. 2, 3; A 2, chpt. 16, 3.
[305] A 2, ch[t. 23, 2.
[306] DN 2, chpt. 2, 3.
[307] DN 2, chpt. 23, 8.
[308] *Ibid.*
[309] *Ibid.*
[310] C 20-21, 9
[311] DN 1, chpt. 1, 12.
[312] DN 2, chpt. 5, 1.
[313] DN 2, chpt. 11, 1.
[314] DN 2, chpt. 10, 1.
[315] DN 2, chpt. 1, 1.
[316] DN 1, chpt. 14, 1.
[317] Moreno, p. 259.
[318] C 20-21,9.
[319] C 3, 63.
[320] C 16, 2.
[321] *S. Th.* I, *q.* 63, *a.* 2, c.
[322] *Censure and Opinion.*
[323] Moreno, p. 264.
[324] C 10, 3.
[325] C 40, 4.
[326] C 16, 6.
[327] C 3, 63.
[328] DN 2, chpt. 15, 1.
[329] C 14-15, 2.
[330] C 16, 10.
[331] DN 1, chpt. 4, 3.

[332] C 20-21,9

[333] DN 2, chpt. 23, 4.

[334] DN 2, chpt. 23, 5.

[335] C 16, 2.

[336] C 20-21,9.

[337] L 3, 63.

[338] L 3, 64.

[339] *Loc. Cit.* 5.

[340] *Ibid.*

[341] *Ibid.*

[342] C 25, 2.

[343] C 25-21,9.

[344] C 25, 2.

[345] DN 2, chpt. 23, 9.

[346] *Fifth Mansion,* 21.

[347] Ps 34:7

[348] C 16, 2.

[349] A 2, chpt. 9, 2.

[350] *Ibid.* chpt. 12, 2.

[351] DN 2, chpt. 25, 4.

[352] L 3, 64.

[353] C 16, 6.

[354] *Ibid.*

[355] L 3, 64.

[356] C 16, 6.

[357] DN 2,chpt. 23, 4.

[358] *Ibid.*

[359] DN 2, chpt. 23, 14.

[360] Moreno, p. 267.

[361] *Life,* 30, 9-10.

[362] *Idem.*

[363] *Life,* 30, 11-13.

[364] *Ibid.* 30, 10.

[365] Jordan Aumann, OP. *Spiritual Theology,* p. 337.

366 *Ibid.* p. 338.
367 *Spiritual Theology,* p. 340.
368 *Ibid.* pp. 340-341.
369 *Spiritual Theology,* p. 344.
370 *Ibid.* p. 345.
371 *Ibid.* p. 346.
372 *Spiritual Theology,* pp. 350-351.
373 *Ibid.* p. 352.
374 DN 2, 23, 4.
375 *Ibid.* 6.
376 C 22, 4.
377 DN 2, chpt. 15, 1.
378 DN 2, cpt. 2, 1.
379 C 14-15, 16.
380 C 22, 3.
381 C 22, 3.
382 DN 2, chpt. 16, 2.
383 C 14-15, 30.
384 C 2, 4-5.
385 A 2, chpt. 11, 9.
386 *Loc. Cit.* 10.
387 *Fifth Mansions,* 1,1.
388 *Ibid.* 5, 4,5.
389 *Idem.*
390 *Idem.*
391 *Life,* 23,2; 28, 4.
392 *Ibid.,* 5,1.
393 *Sixth Mansions,* 6,6.
394 DN 2, chpt. 23, 10.
395 First line of *The Dark Night.*
396 *Loc. Cit.* second stanza.
397 A prologue, 3.
398 A 1, chpt 3, 1.
399 *Loc. Cit.*

400 *S. Th.* I, *q.* 64, *a.* 1, *ad* 3.

401 A 1, chpt. 2, 1.

402 *Ibid.* Also, St. Thomas says this in 4 *Sent. D.* 6, *q.* 1, *a.* 4, *c.*

403 A 1, chpt. 6, 1.

404 DN 2, chpt. 21, 2.

405 DN 2, 21, 3.

406 A 2, chpt. 6, 7.

407 DN 2, chpt. 21, 3.

408 I Pet. 5:9.

409 DN 2, chpt. 21, 4.

410 A 1, chpt. 1, 1.

411 *Loc. Cit.* 3.

412 A 2, chpt. 1, 2.

413 *Ibid.*

414 *Loc. Cit.* 3

415 *Ibid.*

416 DN 2, 21, 11.

417 A 2, chpt. 4, 5.

418 DN 2, 21, 7.

419 DN 2, 21, 11.

420 DN 2, 21, 11.

421 A 2, chpt. 16, 6.

422 A 2, chpt. 11, 8.

423 A 2, chpt 16, 7.

424 A 2, chpt. 17, 9.

425 A 2, chpt. 11, 2.

426 A 2, chpt. 27, 6.

427 *Loc. Cit.* 7.

428 *Loc. Cit.* 7

429 *Loc. Cit.* 10.

430 A 2, chpt. 21, 4.

431 A 2, chpt. 27, 6.

432 *Ibid.*

433 A 2, chpt. 24, 8.

[434] A chpt. 26, 18.
[435] *Loc. Cit.* 9
[436] A chpt. 26, 18.
[437] A 2, chpt. 27, 4.
[438] A 2, chpt. 29, 12.
[439] A 2, chpt. 30, 6.
[440] A 2, chpt. 32, 6.
[441] DN 1, chpt. 2, 7.
[442] C 3, 9.
[443] A 2, chp. 26, 17.
[444] *Precautions,* 13.
[445] *Life,* 25, 22.
[446] *Ibid.,* 18, 5.
[447] *Second Mansion,* 1, 6.
[448] *Life,* 15, 13.
[449] *Foundations,* 10, 11.
[450] *Life,* 31, 4.
[451] C 7, 6.
[452] *Loc. Cit.* 8.
[453] C 2, 3.
[454] *Ibid.*
[455] C 16, 3.
[456] *Loc. Cit.* 2.
[457] A 2, chpt. 22, 11.
[458] *Loc. Cit.* 9
[459] *Precautions,* 13.
[460] *Loc. Cit.* 11.
[461] A 2, chpt. 22, 11.
[462] Loc. Cit. 16.
[463] A 2, chpt. 30, 5.
[464] A 2, chpt. 26, 18.
[465] A 2, chpt. 22, 16.
[466] Loc. Cit. 17.
[467] L 3, 28.

[468] C 40, 3.

[469] C 40, 1.

[470] C 22, 2.

[471] C 27, 2.

[472] L 4, 14.

[473] *S. Th.* II-*IIae, Q* 145.

[474] C 40, 3.

[475] C 20-21, 15.

[476] C 22, 3.

[477] C 25, 5.

[478] C 20-21, 1.

[479] C 24, 5.

[480] Moreno, p. 267-268.

[481] *Ibid.*

[482] C 33, 3.

[483] C 20-21, 9; loc, cit. 15.

[484] C 24, 8.

[485] A 1, chpt. 15, 2.

[486] C 14-15, 9.

[487] C 15-15, 30.

[488] D 2, chpt. 24, 2.

[489] C 22, 3.

[490] C 16, 2.

[491] *Precautions,* 1.

www.ingramcontent.com/pod-product-compliance
Lightning Source LLC
Chambersburg PA
CBHW031259090426
42742CB00007B/521